MW00436584

"*Uncommon* is a powerful and profound book! Caleb is a great influencer and leader and this book will equip you with the resources you need to live an uncommon life."

—Jentezen Franklin, *New York Times* Best-Selling Author, Senior Pastor, Free Chapel, Gainesville, Georgia

"God has ever only used ordinary people to do extraordinary things. *Uncommon* reminds us that we too can impact the world for God's Kingdom if we fully commit our ordinary, common lives to His extraordinary purposes every day."

—Christine Caine, Best-selling author, Founder A21 & Propel Women

"Caleb has been practicing uncommon leadership around the world in many ways. His practical and powerful insights will help you be a part of our global community and be an influencer not just consumer. "Common sense is not very common", Caleb takes the basics of Christian truth and applies them in remarkable ways. You can lead, you have what it takes, you'll love *Uncommon Leadership!*"

—Casey Treat, Senior Pastor, Christian Faith Center, Seattle, Washington

"I have known Caleb Wehrli for many years and have watched him travel the globe working with an array of leaders from different church groups, in different countries. Caleb offers unique insight and leadership perspectives that will both inspire and challenge you at the same time!

I believe this book will be a great tool in the hand of all who read it, and a key leadership resource for people all over the world. I highly recommend Caleb Wehrli and his book, *Uncommon: Leadership Lessons from Around the Globe*."

—Russell Evans, Senior Pastor,
Planetshakers Church, Melbourne, Australia

"There is nothing common about the Christian Faith, for there is nothing common about our God! Caleb Wehrli, an exceptional leader of leaders, with a unique mandate from God outworked in mission and evangelism has crafted and compiled some of the "Uncommon Acts" of extraordinary heroism lived out within the Christian Church across the globe. Caleb is inspiring, and so is his book *Uncommon*. Welcome reader, to your new top ten book for stiring faith within."

—Glyn Barrett, Senior Pastor !Audacious Church,
National Leader of the Assemblies of God in Great
Britain, Manchester, UK

"Leadership teaching, even some really good teaching, is often parochial and, well, Americanized. Caleb Wehrli's new book shatters that mold. *Uncommon* takes a fresh global view of leadership without borders and I recommend it."

—Mark Rutland, Executive Director,
National Institute of Christian Leadership

"In these pages, Caleb Wehrli shares unique leadership truths through a Kingdom perspective that he himself embodies. A man of the nations, Caleb approaches this much talked subject through uncommon lenses. You will find this is not just another western approach to leadership, but a much broader, global and spiritual way of living out our supernatural Kingdom influence in a fallen world.

I met Caleb as he's been living out the message on these pages. The uncommon vision that he is committed to, requires supernatural strategy to fulfill it. In these pages, the author unveils biblical truths of leadership that have allowed him to literally see fruit around the globe as he travels the nations in the name of the Kingdom."

—Teo Hayashi, Founder Dunamis Movement,
Zion Church & The Send Brazil, São Paulo, Brazil

"With so much emphasis on the kingdoms of men, even as believers we tend to lose sight of the Kingdom of God. Ironically the message of the Kingdom of God was the message of Christ and is the heart of this *Uncommon* book. In reading this text you will begin to see a refreshed view of the Kingdom of God that will empower you to let Christ live in and work through your life. Open this book and dive in to something bigger than yourself … truly God is inviting us into Uncommon Kingdom partnerships."

—Marty Sloan, Lead Pastor, Calvary Church,
Naperville, Illinois

"You want the *Uncommon* to be part of your arsenal, for winning in leadership. The favor of God is upon Caleb. He has experienced an extraordinary impact from the uncommon power of the Holy Spirit. He is a gifted leader, who wants to impart the adventure of the supernatural life of the uncommon in your heart. The *Uncommon* book will reveal God's vision of how far you can see, and it will unlock your compassion for the lost. And will release you from the common ordinary existence, to the abundant life God created you to experience."

—Mikel French, Founder, Mikel French Ministries,
Tulsa, Oklahoma

"If you are ordinary you will never stand out in this generation. As the light of the world, we must shine! Being uncommon is the way to achieve relevance in our day and in this hour. My friend Caleb teaches us with excellence and precision the secrets to a different life. An Uncommon Life!"

—Tiago Brunet, Best Selling Author and Conference Speaker, Founder of the Destiny Institute and Casa de Destino, Sao Paulo, Brazil

"*Uncommon* is a timely writing; an essential guidebook for uncommon Christian living and self-leadership during and beyond this new-and-uncommon era that is upon us. Caleb Wehrli has captured what he himself lives and exemplifies, showing us all how we can be devoted and fruitful followers of Jesus Christ, every day. There's gold here!"

—Wayne Crook, Founding Senior Pastor, Sky City Church, Hong Kong

"I always love hearing stories told by people who have actually been there or have been through something. Caleb Wehrli is one of those people that has seen a lot and learned a great deal from what he has seen. He is a remarkably uncommon leader whom I believe you're going to enjoy learning from."

—Dino Rizzo, Executive Director of ARC, Association of Related Churches, Birmingham, Alabama

"Caleb Wehrli provides us with much needed encouragement for these challenging times in his latest book *Uncommon: Leadership From Around the Globe.* Caleb clearly addresses the difficulties we have faced since the outbreak of COVID 19 which have changed the world in which we live. In reading *Uncommon,* we are encouraged by many of Caleb's personal testimonies and those of others. Caleb brings us back to many of the most basic teachings of the Scriptures such as trust, commitment, giving and perhaps the most important during times of trial: peace and love. *Uncommon* is a message for our times. Many in the developed world have enjoyed a long period of comfort which in some cases have led to complicity and a compromised faith. Caleb's message challenges and encourages us to a life of deeper devotion which will result in a powerful manifestation of resurrection power in the life of the follower of Jesus."

—Samuel Smadja, Founder and President of Sar-El
Tours, Elder of Messianic Assembly, Jerusalem, Israel

"I've known Caleb for over ten years, and we have ministered together in many places. So when I read in his book "There is nothing common about living a life full of Jesus" I know that his own life serving God in different capacities around the globe testifies to that fact. Allow God to take you on an uncommon journey as you read this book."

—Sergio Hornung, Senior Pastor,
Iglesia Agua Viva, Lima, Peru

"Uncommon impact is made by common people who choose to live every day with the reality that Jesus is alive within them. Caleb's book resonates so strongly with me because it acknowledges geographical, seasonal and cultural limitations and yet reminds us of the greater reality that transcends them all - the living King and His Kingdom resides within you! Caleb's authentic love for God and people combined with his vast experience on the mission field offers a unique and dynamic perspective that will broaden your vision, stir your faith, and awaken your spirit to live the uncommon life you were always called to live!"

—Mark Varughese, Founder and Senior Leader of Kingdomcity, Author of *Ready Fire! Aim*, Perth, Australia

"Caleb is an uncommon leader! For the past 20 years, I've gotten to see Caleb's leadership first hand on the field and in life. His life has been a series of uncommon experiences because of his commitment to live a life of uncommon, radical faith and obedience to God. I believe the words he's written in this book will be helpful to you. Caleb speaks from a place of experience, and I am a firm believer in what he has to offer."

—Paul Daugherty, Lead Pastor, Victory Church Tulsa

"Unless it's been suppressed, each of us has an innate desire to live extraordinarily. But so often we settle for mediocrity when greatness is within our grasp. In *Uncommon*, you'll be challenged to rise above the norm and empowered to pursue an uncommon life."

—John Bevere, Best-selling Author and Minister, Co-founder of Messenger International

UN
COMMON

LEADERSHIP LESSONS FROM AROUND THE GLOBE

CALEB WEHRLI

Uncommon: Leadership Lessons From Around the Globe
Copyright © 2020 by Caleb Wehrli

Published by Four Rivers Media

All rights reserved. No portion of this book may be reproduced, stored in a retrieval system, or transmitted in any form or by any means—electronic, mechanical, photocopy, recording, scanning, or other—except for brief quotations in critical reviews or articles, without prior written permission of the author.

Scripture quotations marked KJV are taken from the King James Version of the Bible. Public domain. Scripture quotations marked NIV are taken from the Holy Bible, New International Version®, NIV®. Copyright © 1973, 1978, 1984, 2011 by Biblica, Inc.™ Used by permission of Zondervan. All rights reserved worldwide. www.zondervan.com. The "NIV" and "New International Version" are trademarks registered in the United States Patent and Trademark Office by Biblica, Inc.™ | Scripture quotations marked NKJV are taken from the New King James Version®. Copyright © 1982 by Thomas Nelson. Used by permission. All rights reserved. | Scripture quotations marked TLB are taken from The Living Bible copyright © 1971 by Tyndale House Foundation. Used by permission of Tyndale House Publishers Inc., Carol Stream, Illinois 60188. All rights reserved. The Living Bible, TLB, and The Living Bible logo are registered trademarks of Tyndale House Publishers. | Scripture quotations marked NLT are taken from the Holy Bible, New Living Translation, copyright © 1996, 2004, 2015 by Tyndale House Foundation. Used by permission of Tyndale House Publishers, Inc., Carol Stream, Illinois 60188. All rights reserved. | Scripture quotations marked MSG are taken from THE MESSAGE, copyright © 1993, 1994, 1995, 1996, 2000, 2001, 2002 by Eugene H. Peterson. Used by permission of NavPress. All rights reserved. Represented by Tyndale House Publishers, Inc. | Scripture quotations marked GNT are from the Good News Translation in Today's English Version—Second Edition. Copyright © 1992 by American Bible Society. Used by Permission.

For foreign and subsidiary rights, contact the author.

Cover design by: Martijn van Tilborgh

ISBN: 978-1-950718-66-5   2 3 4 5 6 7 8 9 10 11

Printed in the United States of America

DEDICATION

To my Lord and Savior, Jesus Christ, who paid the ultimate price so I can live an Uncommon Life.

To my wife, Sarah, who is the most amazing woman I know, the best preacher I know, and the one who continually challenges me to be more like Jesus through her example.

To my son, Isaac, who is so encouraging and joyful, and who will always be my CHAMP!

To my daughter, Lizzy, who is beautiful inside and out, and loves to do what's right.

To my Dad, who always encourages me to believe BIG and trust God.

To my Mom, who has loved me and prayed for me since my first breath.

To my brother, Shad, who has been there for me and looked out for me.

To my sister, Angela, who has always believed in her little brother.

To my friends in ministry, who continually challenge me to excel and go further than I think I can.

And to all those who read this book, I pray you experience the joy of living an Uncommon Life!

CONTENTS

INTRODUCTION

Our world drastically changed in a matter of a few weeks in March 2020. An invisible pathogen known as COVID-19 rapidly transformed our planet. The results of this global pandemic left our world looking for uncommon solutions to some significant challenges. Yet as believers we know that the answer to every challenge is still found in the person of Christ and His unchanging Kingdom.

In fact, Hebrews 12:28 tells us that in the face of global shaking one thing remains unshakable, unbreakable, and unmovable—Jesus and His Kingdom. Amazingly, this Kingdom has already been deposited in the hearts of everyone who has surrendered their lives to Jesus (Luke 17:21). This means that despite worldwide uncertainty, whether from Corona or some other challenge, that Christ's rule and reign equips you and me with the resources that we need to live uncommon lives.

This looks like embracing a life that places Jesus at the center of everything we do. In other words, Jesus wants to live His life through us! And as we surrender our hearts, He comes to live inside of us and reveal uncommon qualities through us. Some people think that living this kind of life is only for the spiritual elite of our generation. This is simply not true. Every believer is called to live an uncommon life through Jesus' presence living inside of him or her. This is true no matter one's background, education, race or occupation.

This book is about understanding and operating in these Kingdom characteristics that transcend geographical boundaries.

These ideas can be applied to leaders cross-culturally, and I am going to share personal stories of how Jesus taught me these principles as I have traveled around the globe. They will help you understand and release what Jesus has already deposited in your life, so you can make an impact in your context. They include characteristics such as availability, attitude, generosity, pursuit and vision. The cumulative expression of these Kingdom attributes through your life will lead to uncommon living! No matter who you are, what your background is, or what your vocation looks like, if you know Jesus then you already have this uncommon Kingdom alive inside of you. It's time to let it be released through your life in all its fullness.

CHAPTER 1

BEYOND COMMON

At the age of 17, I visited Africa for the first time. It was my very first mission trip, and I signed up to travel to Ghana with a team of other young people from my church in Tulsa, Oklahoma, USA. I was so excited to see what Jesus would do through our team. I expected God to move—through our team leader, through the local contacts, as well as through some of my friends. Much to my shock, God used me—powerfully. It's hard to describe what happens when a teenager stands up in a church service in a remote African village to preach for the first time. The words of truth flowed out of me as if I had been speaking for years. By the end of the service, the entire church responded to the simple altar call.

I'm still not entirely sure what happened that day, but I do know the power of God fell from heaven transforming everyone present—including me. People were saved, others healed and delivered, and everyone experienced a fresh encounter with God. All I know is that in a moment I had stepped out of my ordinary, common teenager life into God's extraordinary, uncommon call on my life. Christ's uncommon Kingdom had been released through my common life. I'm forever grateful for what happened in Ghana because I realized that the needs of our world must be addressed by the uncommon reality of Jesus being expressed through simple people like a 17-year-old teenager named Caleb Wehrli. Since that moment, I have been convinced of one thing: There is nothing common about living a life full of Jesus.

During times of uncertainty, things change quickly. Transition from what was to what will be is not necessarily easy. During such uncommonly challenging times many people yearn to go back to normal. The challenge with this desire is that normalcy is relative. Our so-called normal is often abnormal in light of the person and work of Jesus. To cite one example, is it normal to spend hours daily on social media and only a few minutes in prayer? Or to live for ourselves instead of living the lives that Jesus has planned for us? God often uses seasons of great challenge to get us out of what we think is normal and back into what God calls normal: living like Jesus.

For many of us our normal patterns and habits are far too often abnormal when compared to Jesus and His Word. The current challenges of our world require something more than normal, common Christianity. It's time for the people of God to rise out of the common into the uncommon. This is an hour for our lives to impact a hurting, confused, and searching generation. If Jesus lives inside of you, then you are qualified to live an uncommon Kingdom life. Moreover, you are part of Jesus' plan to transform our world.

Becoming Remarkably Uncommon

One of the definitions of uncommon is "remarkably great." Of course, there are others, but that's my favorite one. What I have learned is that as long as you're connected to a remarkable God, then your life will become just that—remarkable. I mean, think about it for a moment. When was the last time God did something common? Think about creation. Think about the miracles Jesus performed. Think about the intricate design of human bodies and plants and animals and space. If God does everything in an uncommon way, then didn't He create us to be uncommon also? And if we're created in His image, doesn't that mean we're meant to do remarkable, uncommon things?

I love how 1 Peter 2:9 (NIV) describes this idea of being remarkably uncommon. It says, "But you are a chosen people, a royal priesthood, a holy nation, God's special possession, that you may declare the praises of him who called you out of darkness into his wonderful light." Did you catch that? Royal. Chosen. Holy. Special. Sounds pretty uncommon to me!

Jesus illustrates it this way in Matthew 5:14 (NLT): "You are the light of the world—like a city on a hilltop that cannot be hidden." What does light do? It stands out in the middle of darkness. Have you ever seen a city on a hill at nighttime? The streetlights can be seen from far away. Both of these verses prove to us that just by receiving Jesus as your Lord and Savior you have been made remarkable. You are royal, chosen, and called. If you have a relationship with Christ, then you're already started down the path to living an uncommon life. Yet, He wants you to take it further.

Think about people like Reinhard Bonnke, Mother Teresa, Billy Graham, Ravi Zacharias, Amy Carmichael, Martin Luther King, Jr. They are all considered remarkable because their lives left an uncommon mark on their generations. It's not because they were superhuman; rather, they left a remarkable impact because of the uncommon way they approached their common lives. They made a difference in millions of other people because of how they allowed Jesus to be expressed through them in ordinary things, each and every day.

Likewise throughout the Bible, we see men and women who rose to the call to live remarkable lives for God. People like Deborah, Peter, Esther, Paul and Daniel. Most of these people lived in times of great transition and turmoil. It would have been easy to live a complacent, common life. Instead they chose to be remarkable. They made a decision every day to live out the uncommon Kingdom characteristics that propelled them into an uncommon life. The result is that they left an uncommon mark on their generations.

I could talk about more modern examples of people who lived remarkable Kingdom lives. I think of people like T. L. Osborn, Billy Joe Daugherty, and Oral Roberts. Each one of these people lived an uncommon life that left an eternal impact on his generation. Let me briefly mention Oral Roberts and the impact that his life made.

Oral Roberts was one of my childhood heroes. He was one of the greatest healing evangelists of his generation before starting Oral Roberts University, my alma mater. Interestingly, Roberts wasn't an uncommonly great preacher because he was born that way. In fact, he was born into great poverty in central Oklahoma. At the age of 17, he almost died from tuberculosis. However, God miraculously healed him. Furthermore, he faced outspoken criticism from many mainline Christian denominations in his day for daring to proclaim that God still wanted to heal people.

Despite the great opposition and challenges he faced, he lived a remarkable life. During his lifetime he personally laid hands on over 6 million people while impacting the lives of millions of others around the world. He would often say, "God is a good God, and the Devil is a bad Devil." His simple faith witnessed God's power heal, save, and deliver multitudes. Oral chose to live an uncommon life each and every day. And, he never gave up.

The point I'm making is this: *Uncommon impacts are made by common people who choose to live each and every day from the reality that Jesus lives within them.*

As you read this book, I hope you'll go beyond being inspired. I hope you'll let God upgrade your belief system and faith level. Let Him challenge the way you do things. Let Him convince you to leave the normal and never go back. It's time to be uncommon!

The bottom line is that once you get a taste, glimpse, or vision of God's uncommon plan for your life, common just won't work anymore. If He is ready to use teenagers in the sweltering African heat in extraordinary ways, then He is ready to use your life in an uncommon, remarkable way. If you remain satisfied with the common, then you won't be able to live the life you're called to. And you won't have the impact on your friends, family, coworkers, and communities that you are meant to have.

Are you ready to start *your* journey toward uncommon? Good. Then let's start with what I perceive as the beginning of everything uncommon—your personal availability to Jesus and His plan for your life.

CHAPTER 2

UNCOMMON AVAILABILITY

Have you ever wondered how Jesus picked His followers? Have you questioned what *criteria* it was that He looked for in choosing His 12 disciples? I have. I did for a long time, actually. *Maybe it was education,* I thought. *Or maybe it was family background or specific talents or capabilities.* Finally, in West Africa, I got a glimpse of the real answer.

The year was 1995, and I was attending Victory Christian School in Tulsa. As a part of our studies, I was presented with the opportunity to go on a mission trip. I decided to participate, but my reasons were probably not quite as noble as other participants'. I'm sure the thought of changing lives was somewhere in the back of my mind, but I was more intrigued by the fact that a trip to Africa was bound to be an adventurous one. I was excited about safaris and snapping photos of rare wild animals!

I also knew that a lot of pretty girls would be going on this trip (the most beautiful being my wife, Sarah—but we'll save that story for later). I had one idea of what would happen on this trip, but God had another one—a much better one. After a few days of ministering as a group, our leader informed us that we would be changing our ministry focus. A bus was going to drop us off in pairs in different villages. We would be picked up a couple of days later. My ministry partner was a buddy of mine, so my mind was eased to some extent, but not enough to keep me from panicking just a little.

"Nobody knows where we are!" I whispered to him as we unloaded from the bus. "If we die, no one will even know *where* to look for us!" For about an hour, we stood in the middle of this rural village, sweating and nervously looking for our contact. Finally, a very happy-looking man dressed in a suit rode up to us on his bicycle. *How he could be smiling, dressed like that, in 100-degree weather is beyond me,* I thought as he approached. He stopped his bicycle and addressed us.

"It's so good to meet you," he said. "We're glad that you're preaching tonight!"

My friend and I turned to each other in disbelief, looks of fright on our faces. The man seemed unfazed by our reaction explaining that he was the pastor of the village church, and the night service began in approximately 15 minutes. I considered my friend to be somewhat more spiritual than I was, so I looked at him, smiled, and replied to the pastor, "Oh, we are happy to be with you too. I'm glad that my buddy is preaching tonight."

I should've known that he wasn't about to accept a responsibility that big that easily! So, we settled it the only way true, mature Christians settle things—a friendly game of rock, paper, scissors. I'm sure you can guess how the story went. I lost the game, and my first response was complete terror. *I didn't sign up for this! I've never preached a day in my life!* I thought.

The clock was ticking though. There were now just 10 minutes left until the service began. My mind flooded with the thoughts of the villagers' expectations. All they knew was that a "man of God" had come all the way from the United States to deliver a message from God to them. No pressure, right?

Okay, Caleb, you just wasted five minutes freaking out, I told myself.

So, I gathered my thoughts and tried to think of all the great messages I had heard my pastor, Pastor Billy Joe Daugherty, share. I jotted a few notes and then glanced at my watch again. Three minutes! It was then the thought finally hit me to pray, so in those last few minutes, I cried out in desperation to God. He responded by telling me, "Just go. Take your Bible, open the Scriptures, and I'll fill your mouth with the words to say."

With that, I grabbed my Bible and headed inside the small mud hut the people used as their church. There was an African drum on one side and a kerosene lantern on the other. We worshiped together for a couple of hours, and then the pastor called me to come forward. All I remember is opening up my Bible and speaking. I don't remember what scripture I opened to, or what I spoke on. From the moment I opened that Bible until 45 minutes had passed, it was like I was in a time warp—one ending with people kneeling and crying at the front of the altar as I mentioned in the first chapter. It was obvious—God had shown up, and He had shown up big.

After the service ended and the people had trickled out of the hut, I sat at the edge of the platform and wept like a little baby. I had no idea what had just happened. In that moment, I felt the Spirit of God speak to me, "Caleb, what you have is what people need." I sat still for a moment and then responded, "God, I'm 17 years old! I've never done anything like this before. What in the world could I possibly have that people need?"

His response was simple: "My Son."

That was a life-changing moment for me. It proved the truth that I give my life to tell—that God still picks His team the way He always has. He picks those who make themselves available. If you'll make yourself available, without a doubt God will make you capable. And once He makes you capable, you'll be of great use to His Kingdom.

The problem for many of us, including me at 17, is that we have it backward. Most of us think that if we're first capable, we can then be available, and maybe—just maybe—God will use us in big ways. So, we strive hard to be something that we can never be in our own strength. We work hard. We reach hard, and still, we never quite make it.

All of this changes the moment we recognize the power of availability. The moment we decide to clear our schedules, surrender our desires, and exchange our plans for God's. It happens when we fall to our knees in desperation, telling our Father, "I'm done striving. Today, I decide to make myself available for whatever it is that you need." Then and only then is God free to grant us the capability we need to make us eternally useful in His hands.

This process reminds me of what one of my high school buddies went through in order to become a marine. When he first told me of his plans to enlist, I thought, *There is no way.* He wasn't capable. Still, he enrolled and went off to 13 weeks of boot camp. When he returned, he didn't even look like the same person. All of the sudden, his posture was perfect, and so were his manners. He even dressed differently than before. I finally got up the nerve to ask him about it. "Man, what happened to you? Why are you so different?" I questioned.

"It's simple, man," he replied. "I went into that camp a civilian, and I came out a marine."

When my friend made himself available to a new environment and to new instruction, it changed him completely. It made
him capable and ultimately extremely useful to the United States
Marine Corps.

It can be the same for us. *When we make ourselves available
to God, He makes us capable for useful Kingdom service in this life.*
We are all called to be soldiers in God's army. To do so, we have
to go through spiritual boot camp, so to speak. We need to make
ourselves available to His training and leadership so that He can
make us capable and ready to be useful on the frontlines of the
Kingdom. When we choose to live uncommonly available, He will
do uncommon things through our lives to advance His Kingdom.

The Twelve

Let's go back to the calling of the first disciples. In Matthew
14, our story starts with Jesus walking up to some fishermen on
the job. Yet in those men, Jesus saw more than fishermen. He saw
a Kingdom greatness that He knew they didn't see in themselves.
He called out to them, "If you come and follow me, I'll make you
fishers of men." In that moment, those fishermen had a choice,
and they chose to make themselves available. They decided to lay
down their nets—to leave behind the stability of the only life they
had ever known and follow Jesus. And we all know what happened
from there.

That availability is what Jesus desires from us. We may not
see anything special about our lives, but He does. And He wants
to draw it out—to make us capable and useful for His work.
Still, the choice is ours. Will we leave behind the familiarity and
comfort of the past? Will we open ourselves up to the beautiful
uncertainty that comes with walking with Christ? If we wake

up every morning and surrender our lives over to God, He will use us. Sure, He may wreck some of our plans, but we'll be glad that He did.

It's important to realize that the disciples weren't qualified when Jesus called them, and they were well aware of it. In reading the Scripture, we find them having bouts with insecurity, just like I do, and if I'm guessing, just like you do, too. Yet, here's the beautiful truth: God wouldn't call us to a job or position if He hadn't already deposited His limitless Kingdom resources within us to ensure we succeed. Like the disciples, all we have to do is make ourselves available, and He will grace us with the courage, strength, and skill to accomplish His purposes.

If God could use a group of misfit fishermen, zealots, and tax collectors over 2,000 years ago, He can and will use us today. It doesn't matter what our present situations are; He will deliver us out of our messes and make our lives a message of His faithfulness. So, let's get practical. Day-to-day, what does it look like to live available? What does God look for that indicates we are ready to be used? I believe there are three major things we must offer up on a daily basis—our *time*, our *talent* and our *treasure*.

Time represents our focus—what we spend our days doing. *Talent* represents our gifting—the natural skills and abilities God has graced us with. *Treasure* represents what we've been entrusted with—resources that are in our hands. When we choose to make these constantly available to God, He will interrupt our plans with His that are far greater than our own.

Around is not Enough

Since we are discussing what availability is, let's also talk about what it is not. A common misconception is that being *available* is the same as being *around*. In fact, there is a stark difference between the two.

Let's look at the story of the prophet Isaiah. In Isaiah 6:1-9, he overhears God speaking to His angels as He is looking out over the earth. Out of compassion for His people, God asks, "Whom shall I send to declare my truth? Who will go for us?" Since Isaiah was in tune with the Spirit of God, he recognized that this was his moment. He made the decision to make himself available, calling out, "Lord, here I am! Send me." Or, to use a sports metaphor, he yelled, "Coach, pick me! Pick me!"

Just like a fourth grader on a football field, Isaiah didn't raise his hand to ask what qualification or prior experience was needed. He just said he would go. That's the difference between being around and being available. When you're around, people might notice you and ask you to do something, but when you're available and in tune, you ask them. After that encounter, God sent Isaiah to His people and filled his mouth with words to say. He made him capable and ultimately incredibly useful to his generation.

Today, I want to pose this question to you: Are you available or just around? And, I want to encourage you to look deep into your heart for the answer. It's easy to say, "I'm available. I've been available for God to use me for a long time." However, being around the people and things of God is not the same as being available to God. When you truly make yourself available, you'll know it. God's response will leave no uncertainty in your heart.

Pleasant Interruptions

One part of His response is the steady stream of pleasant interruptions that follow our availability. I know what you're thinking:

Interruptions are never pleasant! True enough, but when we make ourselves fully available to God, His interruptions—which we normally would've avoided—actually become something we look forward to.

That's what happened to another man of God whose works are recorded in Scripture—Philip. In Acts 8, we are given a snapshot of his life. He was a preacher, working, serving and doing great things for God. People were being delivered, healed, and saved. A tremendous move of God had broken out in Samaria, but one morning God interrupted Philip's plans for the day with a new directive. An angel said to him, "Philip, go down the road that leads south out of Jerusalem toward the place that is the desert." That was it. That was all of the instruction he received.

Now, I'm going to compare myself to Philip, because I too am a minister, doing the work of God. If God interrupted my message preparation with an instruction to drive down the highway leaving my ministry behind, I'm not too sure what I would think, to be honest. I would probably have some questions like, "Well, why am I going? Who will I talk to? How long will I be gone? What are you going to give me if I go?"

Philip's response was profound. The Bible says simply that he "arose and went." No questions. No objections. He just welcomed God's interruption because He was *that* available. He knew that God's plans would far exceed anything he could've planned. If you read the story, you'll discover that this was a significant Kingdom encounter. Along the desert road, Philip met an Ethiopian eunuch, an official of Queen Candace, struggling to understand the book of Isaiah. When Philip approached him, he asked, "Do you understand what you're reading?" The eunuch replied, "How can I unless someone explains it to me?"

Philip jumped into the chariot with the eunuch and explained how Isaiah's message related to Jesus and then led him into salvation and baptism. In that moment, the Kingdom of heaven collided with the kingdoms of Africa and has been doing so ever since. The eunuch was later used by God to bring the gospel to his entire nation. Who knows how many people would have missed the message of Christ's salvation if Philip hadn't made himself fully available, joyfully welcoming God's interruption?

Making ourselves available is one of the best choices we can make in our Christian lives. Philip did it. Paul did it. The disciples did it. And all were used to make a significant impact in their day. We can have that kind of impact, too. We have to come to the realization that there are people and purpose on the other side of our decision to surrender our time, treasure, and talent. If we choose to make ourselves fully available—not just around—God will use us in a great way.

So, I charge you to make a firm decision—one you won't go back on. Choose to live each and every day available to God. See His divine interruptions as opportunities to make an impact on the lives of those in your path. Don't look back and regret what you could have done; do your part now, and watch what God will do.

CHAPTER 3

UNCOMMON ATTITUDE

A few years ago the Lord spoke to my wife, Sarah, and me about moving to the mission field. At the time, we were content with our lives: a new house, a new baby on the way, a successful ministry. Yet, over the course of the next year the Lord's voice was clear that He wanted us to move to Asia. The day we arrived at our new home—Hong Kong—was an interesting day, to say the least. We didn't know the language. We had no house lined up, no special welcoming committee, and no clue what we would be doing. We had both spent our entire lives in Tulsa. To say that this was a big change for us would be the understatement of the century. We lived in a hotel for two weeks before we found an apartment. We had no plan for how to start a ministry and no person or organization to guide us.

I'll admit that Sarah and I had a few pity parties during that time. We had to constantly remind each other of what God had spoken. Remembering His word would help us recover the Kingdom mindset that we so desperately needed. Amazingly, as we shifted our attitudes, our circumstances started shifting, too. After two weeks of encouraging each other through disappointments, we received a phone call from a lady who planned an outreach to about 200 homeless people. Turns out, all she needed was a preacher. It was an answer to prayer! 65 people got saved that day. That event created a connection with what became our home church in Hong Kong—Sky City Church. As we served there, doors started opening for us to share the gospel across Asia.

From that point on, we hardly stopped! Thousands of people received Christ during our time there. It was in this season that I truly realized the importance of a Kingdom attitude. The concept is basically this: *You may not be able to control your surroundings or your circumstances, but you can always dictate what your response will be.* When we allow our attitude to be controlled by what God says instead of what we see, things start to shift.

Not long ago, I heard about a group of students who had been pulled out of class at the beginning of the school year. They were told that they had been selected as the gifted and talented portion of their class, because the faculty and staff saw great potential in them. As a part of this elite group, they would be taught advanced courses. At the end of that year, the students were tested to see how they had done. The teachers were pleased to see that their plan had worked; the "gifted" students had far surpassed the level of learning of the other students.

This was to be expected though, right? After all, this group was the elite group! Actually, that wasn't the case at all. At the end of the year, one of the teachers called a meeting to tell the students the truth: They had been chosen at random. This was not some sick trick the teachers played to get their test scores up; it was an intentional act to prove a point beneficial for us all. *When your attitude toward something is raised, your result will rise to meet it.*

Now imagine how much more true this is for us as believers. Paul, in the Berean Study Bible, stated it this way: "I can do all things through Christ who gives me strength" (Philippians 4:13).

We have the tendency to think that this verse was written for a sporting event or a difficult exam at school. Instead, Paul wrote this while locked away in a dark, rat-infested, subterranean Roman prison cell. Talk about adopting the right kind of attitude! Jesus lived inside of him, and because of this, he was convinced that he would be able to succeed.

Let me say it again: *Attitude—not circumstance—decides your outcome.* If you raise your attitude, your life will be raised too. This season we are living in is a difficult one. Corona has impacted many people in negative ways. The need for God's people to approach life with a Kingdom attitude has never been greater. Your attitude needs to be based on Christ's reality inside of you—not the fear and uncertainty of the world around you.

What do you see for your life? Do you see what God sees? Do you have His expectations? Have you aligned your perspective with heaven's perspective? Or do you see through the eyes of your circumstances? If you'll adopt a Kingdom vantage point, then like those students, you'll reach heights you never dreamt were possible. I have discovered that more often than not, what we need isn't a new set of circumstances but a new set of eyes.

Attitude is Everything

Winston Churchill said, "Attitude is a little thing that makes a big difference." I say it this way: *Our perspective calls in our promise.* When we live with a good attitude, focusing on what we can control (the attitude) instead of what we can't control (the situation), things work out to a much better end. Philippians 1:6 (NIV) is a popular and fairly straightforward verse. It says, "Being confident of this, that he who began a good work in you will carry it on to completion until the day of Christ Jesus." It's a great promise from God.

I think that there's more for us here than we realize. Let's look at it backwards, because that end result—the *promise*—is what all God's children anticipate. At the end of the verse, we're assured that we can live a purposeful, meaningful life and complete the earthly assignment He has given to us. That's our promise. Now back up a little more, and it says, "He who began a good work in you...."That part is meant to give you *peace*, as you rest in the fact that God is in charge. He who started the work in you always finishes it and finishes it well. Who better to be leading you?

Finally, let's talk about the beginning—the piece that most people leave out. That's our *perspective*. For God to have the freedom to work in people's lives and for that work to be completed, people must live with an attitude of confidence in Christ, even when they don't feel like it. They need to approach life with an uncommon attitude—an attitude that sees, thinks and understands life differently. A life focused on who Christ is inside of us.

Once again think with me about the person who penned this verse in Philippians: the apostle Paul. When Paul was writing this incredible letter to the church in Philippi, he wasn't just writing to encourage others; he was speaking from direct personal experience. At the time of his writing, Paul's future looked pretty bleak. He was in a Roman jail cell for preaching the gospel. What was Paul's crime? He had been trying to obey Christ, and the results were being falsely accused, beaten, persecuted, and locked in chains. It would have been pretty easy for his attitude to turn sour. Instead, Paul experienced peace because he was sure of the promise.

Furthermore, he also understood the power of his *perspective*. He understood that he needed an attitude of confidence in God and faith in His promise. He knew that things didn't have to be perfect for him to live with the right outlook. If we would see through God's eyes, we would see our situation as Paul did, from a much higher vantage point. Paul knew that if he would raise his attitude, his circumstances would eventually rise to meet it.

It's no surprise then that we read just a few verses later Paul writing confidently, "For I know that this is going to turn out for my deliverance through your prayers and the provision of the Spirit of Jesus Christ." When things get hard, do you maintain this kind of attitude? Do you walk around saying, "Look how big my problem is!" or do you walk around praising, saying, "Look how big my God is! He will use this for my good!" Obviously, it's much easier said than done, but Paul gives us a great plan for walking in this kind of Kingdom perspective in Philippians. How did he do it? There are several steps.

The first is *prayer*. There is no greater tool in life for a Christian than this. Prayer is so powerful because it is direct communication with our Creator—the One who knows all. Paul starts off this letter by reminding the church in Philippi that he regularly prays for them from his prison cell (1:3). Again, in verse nine, he talks about his prayer life. Paul's prayers helped him see what God saw.

The second key is *provision* from the Spirit. There's a certain strength that comes from living in the Spirit. There's a peace that surpasses all understanding that only comes from heaven (Philippians 4:7). And the best part is that this peace is available in every aspect of life—our marriages, families, finances, businesses, health—everything! Romans 8:11 says that the *same* spirit—not a smaller than, mini-me, counterfeit version. The *same* spirit that raised Christ from the dead lives in you and in me. That is a pretty good reason to have confidence!

The final step to choosing an uncommon attitude is found just a few chapters later, in Philippians 4:4. In the middle of his suffering, Paul writes, "Rejoice in the Lord always; again, I will say, rejoice!" In the midst of his darkest hour, he knew that his victory lay in *praise*. When he chose the uncommon route—an attitude of victory in a time of defeat—he confused the enemy. That's what uncommon living does. It confuses the enemy. When you should be down, you're not, and that drives the devil crazy. Even more, it opens the door for God to work.

So, next time life throws something your way, stop and remind yourself of your part—pray, seek the provision of the Spirit, and praise. There's tremendous power in your ability to focus on God, even when things aren't going your way.

Our Biggest Enemy

Now that we've discussed our battle plan, let's talk about one of the main enemies we'll need to fight: disappointment. It's the most common weapon the enemy uses to destroy your faith and distract you from your goal. Disappointment sets you at a crossroads—one at which you can either choose the path of self-focus or God-focus. There, you can surrender to your disappointment or you can surrender your disappointment to God. You can pity yourself, or you can praise.

When discussing self-pity, several people probably enter your mind. That's because you can spot a pity party from a long way away! And if we're honest, more times than not, that's one party we all do our best to avoid. It's not because we're trying to be rude, but because negativity is no fun. A bad attitude is never a joy to be around. What's interesting is that when you talk to such people, you can usually trace their negativity back to a moment or a series of moments in which they were disappointed. Maybe it's the moment they felt abandoned and rejected or found out they were ill. At the crossroads of disappointment, they chose the road of self-focus instead of God-focus, and now their life seethes with doubt and cynicism.

That's not how God intends for us to live. When we allow discouragement to take root in our hearts, it leads us down a slippery slope of constantly missing God's best. It affects our thoughts, which affect our actions, which end up affecting our entire lives. It separates us from God-appointments. God appoints and directs, but when our focus is on our hurts instead of on His goodness, we can't see which way to go.

How is your attitude today? If it's negative, try tracing it back to a specific moment. Maybe it was the loss of your job, a failed relationship, a crisis, or an argument. Now, see that situation for what it is—a simple bump in the road on this amazing journey God has you on. Focus on shifting your attitude back toward God's perspective. As your thoughts change, your words change, and as your words change, your actions will change. Soon enough, your entire life will be transformed.

The tough thing about life is that people *will* disappoint us. It just happens. That's why our hope is not supposed to be in them, but in the One who created them. Paul tells us simply in Romans 5:5 (NLT), "This hope will not lead to disappointment." He also tells us in Romans 8:28 (NIV), "We know that in all things, God works for the good of those who love him, who have been called according to His purpose." Guess what *all* means in the original translation? *All.* Guess what it means in Greek, Spanish, English, German, Russian, and Chinese? *All.* He seriously means *all*—as in everything! As you love God and pursue His purpose for your life, He promises to work *all* things out for your good. He's setting everything up for a future better than anything you could've imagined.

I often picture God's work in our lives like a construction job. Some days, I'll drive home and see a pothole in the road that needs filled. The next morning, I'll drive back the other way and see it fixed! It wasn't magic; it was someone laboring during the night. It was someone working when I couldn't see. It seems like it happened all of a sudden, but it didn't. It was taken care of because someone was there behind the scenes addressing the matter. That's exactly how God works in our lives. He addresses situations often when we're unaware of it. He's covering our pasts and preparing our futures, even while we're asleep. When we see life that way, it becomes much easier to adopt an uncommon attitude.

Uncommon Results

Attitude is like the process of sowing and reaping. When you sow an uncommon attitude, you'll reap uncommon results. You may not be able to choose what situations life gives you, but your response is always your choice. Not so long ago I visited a member of our church in the hospital. His story reminded me of this truth.

Ten years previously, he had inhaled some bad chemicals on his job site. About 50 percent of his lungs deteriorated in just 15 minutes. He visited the doctor and received his prognosis: just 10 months to live. At that time, he lived in a northern American state, so he decided that if he had less than a year to live, he was at least going to move south and avoid the harsh winter. He moved to Orlando, FL. He began to spend his time praying, trusting God, and believing His Word. Every time the doctor would give him a negative report, he would choose to keep his confidence in God.

He consistently chose an uncommon attitude—one that was persistent in prayer, Spirit-provided strength, and praise. When you talked to him, you instantly knew you were talking to a man *filled* with joy. He was one of those people who encouraged *others* even when he was in his toughest of times. This man chose an uncommon attitude, and in turn, he received uncommon results. He lived 15 years past his diagnosis. Not months—*years*.

When we keep our focus fixed on the magnitude of our God over the size of our problems, our life's story will be uncommon.

CHAPTER 4

UNCOMMON LANGUAGE

Don't mix bad words with your bad mood." I can still hear this phrase ringing through the classroom, as I tried hard to keep my eyes from rolling in annoyance. At the school I attended, our teachers were big on watching "your words." Though I didn't like the discipline at the time, positive, faith-filled speech has proven to be one of the most constructive things I learned there. Years later, on a trip to Peru, the truth about the power of our words was further cemented in my heart.

My wife and I had brought our church's youth team to minister in this beautiful country. We flew into the capital city and continued our travels up the Amazon River to minister in some of the villages. We made a stop at a small store to get drinks. Just as we were boarding the boat to continue our journey, a woman ran up to us, yelling in Spanish.

"I heard you guys are a church group! Please, would you come pray for my son?" she asked. We didn't have much time, but we decided to go with her. As we walked towards her home, she told us that he had contracted malaria several weeks earlier and was now on the verge of death. As we continued walking, she requested we take him to the hospital and pray for him there. We knew that was too far out of our way, and to be honest, we were confident that God didn't need us to escort him to the hospital in order to heal him.

So, I spoke boldly, "God's just going to heal him at your house, okay?"

She nodded. As we entered the room, we could see the boy was dying; it was obvious the malaria had infiltrated his whole body. It was over 100 degrees outside, but his body was reacting as if it were a frigid 30 degrees inside. He was both shaking and sweating profusely.

The team gathered around, laid hands on the boy, and prayed. We didn't pray for him for hours. We didn't even shout. We just made a simple Bible-based declaration of his healing. After we finished, we gathered up our team and rushed back to the boat so that we could head to our final ministry site. Amazingly, the lady ran after us: "Please, come look at my son, now!" she exclaimed.

It hadn't even been five minutes since we had left, but she was obviously overcome with emotion, so we turned around. When we got to the room, we were amazed. The sick, sweaty boy was not shaking or convulsing anymore; instead, he was walking around, talking plainly as if nothing had ever been wrong. What had affected his body for two weeks was reversed in just a few minutes—not because we were some big-time faith evangelists, but because we recognized the power of uncommon language. Here's the reality. Our words can produce miracles—and not just in our bodies, but also in our relationships, in our finances, in our health, and in every part of our lives that we choose.

Seeds

One of the best word pictures I've heard relating to our speech is an agricultural one: the process of sowing and reaping. Here's why. After seeds are sown, they first take root; then, they produce fruit. The words we sow into our lives follow the same process. So, when we see a fruit we don't like—a temper, a bad financial situation, or a strife-filled relationship—we must go back and examine the seed that took root. What words had we spoken over ourselves? What had we declared over the situation?

No situation is too hard to remedy when we begin to see challenges through this lens. The good news is that no matter how many bad seeds we've planted, we can always uproot the fruit and start over again. So today, ask yourself: What seeds are you sowing over yourself, your family and your spouse? What kinds of seeds are taking root regarding your health, your finances, and your career? Are you using common language, speaking only what you see in the natural? Or, like Romans 4:17, are you using uncommon language—calling things that are not yet as though they are.

When we choose to sow seeds of uncommon language, we reap an uncommon, abundant harvest. *It's hard to live in victory when you're talking defeat. So, let your words lead you toward your destiny, not your demise.* If you don't know what to say, let God speak for you. Grab your Bible and write down what He has to say about your life and your future. You can never go wrong by speaking Scripture! It's just like Deuteronomy 32:47 says, the words of the Bible are more than mere, idle words—they are your *life*.

The Good Ole Days

"I remember the good ole days." How many times have you heard that comment? Whether it's in conversation with our parents, grandparents, old classmates or new friends, it's easy to spend our time focusing on past memories. The problem is that it often leaves us feeling less than content with the present. One of the worst things we can do is buy into the lie that as life goes forward it goes from good to worse, because, with God, it's always meant to get better. It's just as Proverbs 4:18 (NIV) says, "The path of the righteous is like the morning sun, shining ever brighter till the full light of day."

Just as focusing on yesterday's great moments can steal from today, so can over-focusing on today's challenges steal our tomorrow. If our thoughts and words center around what we're dealing with *today*, we'll never be prepared for *tomorrow*. But if we'll focus on sending faith-filled words ahead of us, they'll begin preparing our tomorrow. There's no question that life will bring many trials and tribulations. The Bible actually says that in the last days, things will get very dark. That doesn't mean our lives have to be that way though! Christ's light on the inside of us is brighter than any and every dark thing. Even in the midst of a dark *today*, we can call forth the bright and beautiful *tomorrow*.

Called to Create

In Genesis 1, we read how God created an entire, beautiful world simply by using His words. I think that is a beautiful picture of how God designed our lives. He gave us the creative power to design our world with our words. Proverbs 18:21 (ESV) says that "death and life are in the power of our tongue." If He has given us the power to create what happens in our world, why wouldn't we send our words in a positive direction? Why wouldn't we create a world we want to live in? Please understand that God doesn't grant us this creative power so that we can create whatever we want, whenever we want; He gives it to us so that we can play a part in seeing His promises for our lives come true. As we speak in faith the many promises from His Word, He will be faithful to perform them.

Just as easily as we can create positive changes, we can also create a negative world with the words we speak. If we constantly talk about how terrible work is going, how bad our marriage is, or how sick we feel, those things will start to take root and produce fruit in our lives. And that fruit not only affects us, but it also affects the lives of those around us, hindering our witness with them. Not convinced that your speech affects others? Just think about that one person at work, at your child's sporting event, or at the grocery store that you always seem to avoid. Why do you do that? It's probably because you don't feel better when you leave him or her; in fact, you usually feel worse. And more than likely it's because of the words that person chooses to speak. They don't create positive things based on God's promises. They create negative things based on fears and disappointments.

When we choose common words—words that simply describe our view of our situation—we find ourselves caught up in a repetitive cycle of negativity. But when we choose words that are uncommon—words that describe what God sees above what we currently see—we create an attractive, positive environment.

God Is on Your Side

No two people in the Bible understood this reality better than Joshua and Caleb—two Israelites God used to bring His promises about for His people. Here's what happened. After the Israelites fled Egypt, they wandered in the wilderness for years. When they finally arrived near the Promised Land, Joshua and Caleb were two of 12 spies Moses chose to investigate the land. They were instructed to find out what the Israelites were up against.

It's important to point out that all 12 of these men were considered the best of the best among the Israelites, the smartest and most talented of them all. Moses must have been certain that together they could form a strategy that would bring victory. They entered Canaan as a team, but when they returned, two different reports surfaced.

10 reported something like, "This land is amazing, but there are huge giants and walled cities. We will surely die if we try to take the land God has promised us." Joshua and Caleb had a different perspective. Their response was in the minority. It was different—uncommon, because they focused on the promise instead of the problem, and they remembered Who was on their side.

They said, "This land is amazing, and yes, there are huge giants and walled cities, but God has given us this land, so let's go and take it." Now, let's think about this for a minute. Those 12 people all looked at the same walls. They saw the same giants. They had received the same promise from God, but one group focused on the problem instead of God's power to accomplish the promise. One group had forgotten Who was on the people's side.

It's possible that I can face the same issue as my friend, be promised the same outcome as he, and still receive a different result. Why? Uncommon language produces uncommon results, but common language leaves it up to circumstance. We have an incredible advantage over every problem we'll ever face: We have the Creator of the universe on our side. Why would we *not* choose to be on the team that always wins?

The Faith Connection

One day, not long ago, I received a call from a friend in the middle of a devastating time. One of his children had been born prematurely, and the doctor had said that she wouldn't make it through that first night. And, if by some miracle she did, she would be severely brain-damaged, never able to live a normal life. As a father, my heart broke for my friend, but it didn't take long before his speech revealed something promising.

"So, that's what the doctor said," he concluded after giving me the detailed prognosis. He breathed in deeply, and with a smile that I could hear, he continued, "However, I don't believe it. I believe that my daughter is going to make it. And not just make it—eventually be totally healthy."

My friend went on for 15 minutes, giving me scripture after scripture about what God had promised him. He was sure that if Jesus could heal people back in the Bible days, He could heal his daughter today. It became evident that he wasn't going to settle for anything less than all that God had for him and his family. He sowed seed after seed of faith into his daughter's future. If you've been around that kind of faith before, you know that it is contagious. It wasn't long before I started chiming in, speaking the same things into existence. At the end of the conversation, our faith was strong. We were excited about watching this miracle unfold.

At about seven o'clock the next morning, I received a text from my friend. His daughter had made it through the night. We celebrated together with a steady stream of "Thank you, Jesus!" and "He is faithful!" Then, by about noon, I received another text. "The doctors can't find anything wrong. We're headed home."

We celebrated again, thanking God that He is always committed to honoring our faith—faith that "believes" and so it "speaks" as 2 Corinthians 4:13 says. Uncommon language is a natural response to a heart overflowing with faith. When we build our confidence up so much that we can't help but speak God's promises over our lives *even* when it seems impractical, He will reward us.

Fear Less

Talking about having faith and speaking life is much easier than living it out, so let's close this chapter by getting practical. If there is one step you can take today that will push you in the right direction, it's to fear less. Just as much as faith can fill one's speech, so can fear. In every situation, we choose between two roads to travel down—the road of fear and the road of faith. We can't walk down both at the same time; we have to choose one or the other. It's only on the road of faith that we can watch the impossible become possible right before our eyes.

One of my favorite ways to conquer fear is through praise. When you thank God in faith for what He is going to do, it builds up your spirit. Pretty soon, your faith overtakes the very doubt you once felt so deeply. Another way to fear less is to see fear for what it really is—selfishness. What do I mean? Selfishness tells us that the battle is *ours* to fight, but faith reminds us that it's not ours at all. It's *God's*. When we surrendered our lives to Him, we also surrendered our battles. Therefore, when we fear, we're actually operating in selfishness, trying to control the outcome of a battle we were never meant to fight. Do you want to be selfish with God? I don't!

Now, don't get me wrong. I'm not naïve. I know that we may never be able to live 100 percent fearlessly, but I do believe that every day, we can choose to fear less. Every time we walk into a situation we can say, "Today, I am going to choose faith over fear. I am going to stop the lies of the enemy from overtaking my mind, and I am going to speak the promises of God into existence." The next time fear knocks at your door, let faith answer. Remember that you can walk and talk differently because of Christ's presence living inside of you!

So, if your words create your world, what kind of world are you living in? Are you happy with it, or is there room for improvement? I challenge you today to take inventory of what seeds you're planting. Choose those of faith, not fear. Don't settle for speaking common words that simply describe your situation. Speak into existence the fruit you want to see! You were made for uncommon language because you were made to be uncommon.

CHAPTER 5

UNCOMMON GENEROSITY

After dozens upon dozens of trips across the world, I am convinced: After one trip to a third-world country, your perspective on generosity will be challenged and changed. It happens to me almost every time I go. I'll never forget one instance in a small rural village in Tanzania. At the end of my sermon, a lady and her children approached me carrying a bunch of fruits and vegetables. It was all they had to give for their offering, and they graciously gave everything. I witnessed the same thing in Nepal. I was sharing about the things God was doing in Southeast Asia through various outreaches, when the pastor stopped me.

"We, as a church, want to help buy presents for kids in Southeast Asia. We may not be able to go help, but we can send money." So, they took up an offering right then and there! It was one of the most beautiful sights to see—people who hardly had anything to give, giving sacrificially to help others in need. These people truly understood the meaning of real generosity. Why are people naturally drawn toward generosity? It's because when they're around generous people, they just feel better! When we know that people love us enough to sacrifice for us, we want to be near them.

God showed us the most generous act of love in the history of the world when He gave His one and only Son to die for our sins.

If you're a parent, can you imagine sacrificing your only child for people who may never even choose to accept your love? It would be tough. Even when we don't accept His generosity and even though we're unworthy of it, God still gave everything. Romans 5:8 (NIV) says, "While we were still sinners, Christ died for us." While we were still running from God, He saved us. He loved us. He gave His very best for us. Generosity is at the core of who Christ is. His whole life speaks of sacrificial generosity. He wants it to be at our core, too.

In John 6, we're shown another example of what happens when generosity pervades people's lives. Jesus was preaching to over 5,000 people. He had been sharing all day, so the people were getting hungry. After a while, He turned to one of His disciples, Philip, and asked him to feed the people. Phillip was shocked, so he asked in verse 5, "Where shall we buy bread for these people to eat?" He responded accurately, but with no faith, "It would take more than half a year's wages to buy enough bread for each one to have a bite!" That's when, in verse 9, Andrew, another disciple, spoke up. "Here is a boy with five small barley loaves and two small fish, but how far will they go among so many?" he asked.

After listening to His friends, Jesus had everyone sit down. He took the five loaves and two fish that the little boy had generously offered him. He prayed a prayer of thanks for the food and then instructed the disciples to distribute it to the people. When everyone had eaten their fill, He sent the disciples to collect the leftovers. There were 12 baskets full. I like to think that Jesus intentionally made sure there were 12—one for each of the disciples—to remind them that true faith gives Him space to work.

The disciples weren't the only ones who learned a lesson that day; the little boy did too. He could have thought, "I had better keep my food. There're too many to share with around here. And besides, Mom told me to eat it all." I'm sure he could have found many reasons not to share. But He didn't. He gave in faith, trusting that God would use his meager portion to provide for a multitude. And that is exactly what happened. Though he didn't have much to offer, Jesus took what he surrendered, multiplied it, and used it in a great way.

It's the same for us. *The only direct control we have over our future is the seed we sow in the present through generosity.* When we give, He gives more. Uncommon generosity will always unlock an uncommon storehouse.

What's in Your Hand?

So now, I want to ask you: What's in your hand to give? What are you holding onto that God wants you to be generous with? There are three things I want us to consider when answering this question.

#1—*It doesn't matter how much you have.* No gift is too small for God to use. When we give with pure motives, He will always multiply it for His purposes.

#2—*Generosity isn't just about giving money.* While that's certainly a resource we can use to bless others, it's not the only one. Local church leaders appreciate people who are generous with money for sure because it helps pay the sanctuary mortgage, it allows churches to give to missions, and it enables them to effectively reach out to their communities. It's also important, though, to be incredibly grateful for those who are generous with other resources—talents, time, prayers, and even attitudes like persistence, love, and grace.

I know I am grateful for the person on stage playing guitar, the individuals serving in the nursery, and the teens volunteering in the media department. You know that in order for God's work to be done effectively, it takes all of God's people living generously with what is in their hands.

And, #3—*When you give, you will be blessed.* Proverbs 11:24-25 (NLT) says, "Give freely and become more wealthy; be stingy and lose everything. The generous will prosper; those who refresh others will themselves be refreshed." Proverbs 19:17 (NLT) promises, "If you help the poor, you are lending to the Lord—and he will repay you!" When we are kind to those who are less fortunate, God sees it as service to Him, and He rewards us for our generosity. Though this is encouraging, it should never be the motive for our giving.

Sometimes, God will reward us financially. Sometimes, He will reward us with a new relationship or maybe a promotion into new authority. On earth, He has many different ways to bless us. Sometimes, however, we will never know our full reward until we reach heaven. Here's what I mean. Generosity connects people in a unique way. When you give, your gift often outlives you. It reaches many more people than you could've ever reached on your own. Your life ends up touching more people than you will probably ever know while here on the earth.

Let me give you an example. Our ministry partners with a woman who has served in Thailand for over a decade. She felt God leading her to help children who had been abandoned, abused, and sold into slavery. Every month, she rescues several children caught up in the treacherous cycle of sex trafficking. After a few years of faithful obedience, she was given the opportunity to buy several acres of land on the border of Thailand and Myanmar. Partners of our ministry gave so that she could build houses for the kids, feed them and train them in the ways of God. Not only does this amazing woman receive the eternal reward for her generosity, but so does every person who contributes generously to help her.

We bless the woman, who blesses the children, who in turn will bless their children and grandchildren, as well as many others they will come into contact with. And, when we all enter heaven, I know that they will run up to us with huge smiles on their faces, thanking us for our generosity. That's the way God works. When we give to help someone, we become part of everything that he or she does and every person that is reached. When we are generous, we reap uncommon eternal rewards.

God's Heartbeat

As a follower of Christ, my life's goal is to know His heartbeat—to love whom and what He loves. I want my heart to break when His does. I want my heart to be filled with joy when His is. The more I get in sync with His heartbeat, the more I realize how simple it is. *God's heartbeat is people.* It doesn't matter if they're down-and-out or high-and-up, His heart is to reach people in all spheres and in all stages of life with His love. This takes uncommon generosity. The reality is that living generously can absolutely change someone's destiny. It can radically alter the direction of his or her life. Just think about your own for a moment. At some point, someone somewhere invested something in your life to help you get where you are today. It could have been time, money, or talent.

Just as someone helped you in a time of need, so you are called to help others. That's what the Church is built on. That's what every believer is called to be about. As we represent our Father, we should be known as people with big hearts and open hands. When we allow God to work through us, people will be attracted to Him by the love we show.

When I was in Ecuador several years ago, I was reminded of how much generosity can change not just one life, but several. My wife and I had taken a small group of youth with us and were doing an outreach in a public park. We put on dramas and took turns talking to the people about Jesus. At the end, we gave an altar call, and a woman responded with her two children. As one of the girls on our team prayed with her, she asked, "Why are you here?" The girl was caught off guard and stumbled around for an answer. "Umm.... Well, those are my leaders over there. They brought us. We just want to share Jesus."

The lady's eyes stayed fixed on the girl's face. "No. Why are you here?" she asked again. The girl searched for another answer that might satisfy the inquisitive woman. Again, the lady asked her question, staring at the girl the whole time. Finally, the girl, feeling exasperated, replied, "Ma'am, I'm not sure I know what you're asking."

The lady responded, "I know why you're here. You're here because of me." The girl was a bit confused, so she called us over, so the woman could tell her story. It went like this. That morning, she had woken up to her husband packing his things. He yelled that he was leaving the family for good as he walked out the front door. She had been distraught and full of worry all morning, wondering how she was going to take care of her children alone. So, she grabbed the two kids and told them that they were going on a walk.

As they walked, she cried out to God, "God, if you're real, send someone to me right now to show me that you exist!" Just as she was finishing her supplication, she came upon our group in the park. She stopped to listen and immediately knew that God had sent us just for her. Because our team was uncommonly generous by traveling to Ecuador to share Jesus' love, the lives of that woman, her two children, and many others were changed. Seeing generosity this way makes it all worth it.

When we live with uncommon generosity we see life through a different lens. We don't see our gift as something lost but as something sowed because we know that our gift will live on. It will touch people for generations to come, and in turn we will reap an eternal reward. You know you're operating in uncommon generosity when you no longer see with singular vision. When you look at one hurting person, you see that person but you also see an entire office, workplace, family, city and community that can be reached through that individual.

You also know you're operating in generosity when you possess a deep gratitude for Jesus' gift of salvation. When you live in that constant state of thankfulness, it is only natural to steward the life you've been given by making it count for others. If you struggle to give joyfully, try acting as if you're giving directly to God, blessing Him for all of His invaluable blessings in your life. It makes it much easier to give when you're reminded of all He has given to you. The truth is that God loves every single person on this earth, and He has a plan for each one. People are the reason that Jesus came and died. People are the reason He was raised from the dead. And, people are the reason each one of us exists—to spread the gospel of Christ that is *love*.

Practiced, Not Just Promised

We can easily promise to operate in this kind of love; it's when we actually have to practice it that things can get tough. Jesus knew it would be, which is why He set the standard for us in John 13:34 (NIV). He said, "As I have loved you, so you must love one another."

As I Have Loved You

Uncommon generosity is all about learning to love others how Jesus loves us. As followers of Christ, we're not only called to gather together to praise, preach, and pray, but also to love each other well by loving like Jesus. We're meant to put love into practice—not just into empty promises.

A few Christmases ago, our church sent its first missions team to the country of Cambodia in Southeast Asia. The average person in this country lives on only $50 a month. Can you imagine that? That's less than $2 a day. While there, my wife Sarah felt a strong desire to build a home for children who had been orphaned. She had neither resources nor knowledge of how to build it, but she did have a spirit of generosity and the faith to make it happen. Sarah began sharing God's heart for the project, and within 10 days, she had raised all the money to build the first home. Today, there is not just one home, but *20* homes throughout Southeast Asia, helping to meet the practical, spiritual and emotional needs of those children.

Friends, that's what the gospel is all about. God is looking for people whose lives demonstrate to Him, "If you give it to me, I'll give it." Think about the last time you gave to someone in need. How did it make you feel? When I choose to give individually or collectively with my church family, we become the hands and feet of Jesus, and I feel fully alive. And to me, that's the only way to live.

So how do you want to live? Fully alive, loving others with Christ's generous love? Not just making empty promises, but actually practicing love? Making a lasting difference in the lives of others? If so, I encourage you—whatever you have in your hand, give it to God right now. Generously offer it up to be used by Him, and don't be surprised when it turns into something greater than you could've imagined.

CHAPTER 6

UNCOMMON VISION

Close your eyes. Think about your life 10 years from now. What do you see? What do you see for your family? For your finances? For your health? Now, do you think those things you're imagining line up with what God sees for you? If so, you've got one extremely important trait of the uncommon life down—uncommon vision. This trait allows you to see things from God's perspective. It helps you see a strong marriage, even when it may be struggling. It allows you to see your business succeeding even when finances are tight. I know it may not make sense at first, but that's because *uncommon vision isn't about what we see in the natural. It's about what we see when our eyes are closed.*

Let's think back to our story of Joshua and Caleb—the two spies who kept an uncommon attitude about the Promised Land. When the other spies reported what they saw with their natural eyes, Joshua and Caleb reported what they saw with their eyes closed. In other words, they saw what God saw. When we live like Joshua and Caleb—with uncommon vision—our lives will look and feel different, not just to us, but also to those around us. When others realize that what we see is different, it draws them toward the One who sees everything clearly.

Jesus always sees more in and for us than we see about ourselves. I'll never forget the day this truth was ingrained in my heart. I was on a trip with my wife, Sarah, her sister, Ruthie, and her father, Pastor Billy Joe Daugherty. We were in the capital city of Freetown, Sierra Leone, on the way to a huge crusade, where my father-in-law would speak. A few minutes before we pulled up to the site, Pastor looked over at us and said, "I'm going to be going on to another town tonight. You guys have the service in Freetown."

I'm sure our expressions revealed what our minds were thinking, *Are you crazy?* I know mine did because it eventually came out of my mouth! Pastor simply laughed and said, fully convinced, "Caleb, you three have what it takes. I see it in you." As we walked up onto the stage, I'm sure people were thinking, *Why are there a bunch of kids up there?* Someone came with two microphones and handed them to us, so we could speak.

"Aren't you going to introduce us?" I asked, stalling for more time. He laughed. "We don't need to introduce you. No one knows who you are!" He had a good point! When I got up there, I closed my eyes for a few seconds and remembered my father-in-law's words: "You have what it takes. I see it in you." I tried hard to envision what he saw. As I preached that night, I truly felt a power welling up from Jesus' love for others deep inside of me that I had never known existed. God moved greatly during that service—not because I was a good preacher. He moved because I had chosen to see myself with uncommon vision—the way Jesus and my father-in-law saw me.

Proverbs 29:18 (KJV) says, "Where there is no vision the people perish." When there's no dream, hope or revelation for our lives, they go nowhere. Without a clear direction for our marriages, they will probably end up in divorce. If there's no clear hope for our finances, we may very well end up in bondage. If there's no clear picture of our health, we can easily become sick. Once we get a clear vision, however, it inspires life-changing passion, which leads to inspired action. *Uncommon vision is the beginning of a lifelong road of victory.*

Close Your Eyes

Just like I experienced on that stage, we see uncommonly when we close our natural eyes and see with our spiritual eyes. Acts 2:17 says that God wants to pour out His Spirit on all people, and when He does, we will begin to see things beyond the way they look in the natural. How encouraging that in a world full of despair and calamity, we have hope because we can see what God sees. Sure, what we see in the natural matters, but what we see in the spiritual realm matters even more. That's because as Isaiah 55:8-9 (NIV) says, "For my thoughts are not your thoughts, neither are your ways my ways," declares the Lord. "As the heavens are higher than the earth, so are my ways higher than your ways and my thoughts than your thoughts."

People with uncommon vision see promises instead of problems. They see opportunities in obstacles. They see supernatural intervention in the middle of natural challenges.

Children are the best at seeing uncommonly because they're used to letting their imaginations run wild. Not long ago, my own kids reminded me of this. We were living in Oklahoma at the time. It was winter and snowing too much. The kids were definitely over the persistent snow. They wanted the sun to come back out so that they could swim. My wife and I heard about their summer ambitions continually.

In an effort to encourage them that warm weather was on its way, one afternoon, my wife told them that we would go to the beach sometime after the season had changed. It worked. They squealed with delight and jumped up from the floor and out of their pity party. Sarah was happy that her plan had worked. She went back to doing what she had been doing when she heard footsteps run into the living room.

She went to where our children were and saw Isaac and Lizzie standing there in their swimsuits with a beach bag filled with their towels, sunscreen, and pool toys. "We're ready for the beach, Mom!" they exclaimed when she walked in. Sarah's heart sank when she realized she'd have to burst their bubble. "We're not going to the beach, *now*," she explained. "But the time will come sooner than you think."

Their faces fell. They looked so discouraged. Then Lizzie, who was about five at the time, grabbed her towel, spread it on the floor and laid herself down on it. "What are you doing, Lizzie?" Sarah asked her. "Did you not hear me? We aren't going to the beach yet."

"It's okay, Mommy," her sweet voice responded. "I'm just imagining I'm already there." How powerful would it be, if we all would take this stance spiritually? I strongly believe that if we would "imagine we're already there," our promise would come "sooner than we think." Clearly, Lizzie understood the power of vision—the power of seeing things as they *will be* before they *are*. In the same way, you and I receive promises from God. Promises of a different reality than our current one—where we are healed, prosperous, loved and accepted. Promises that tell us that our children will come back to Christ, our marriages will be strong, and our lives will have purpose.

Even though you may not have obtained the end result yet, I want to encourage you to take Lizzie's stance. Act like you're at the beach in the middle of a snowstorm. See your life for what it can be tomorrow, not just for what it is today. When you get a glimpse of what Christ has in store for you, you won't want to go back to seeing any other way. Jeremiah 29:11 encourages that God knows the plans He has for us, and they're plans to prosper us, not to harm us, plans to give us hope and a future. That's the foundation of uncommon vision! Yet it's only the foundation. Just because God has a plan doesn't mean it'll automatically come to pass. We have a part to play, and it goes beyond imagination.

Live on Purpose

I've heard it said that *everyone ends up somewhere, but few end up there on purpose.* Living on purpose is a choice, and it's kind of like playing a game of darts. When you play, you throw the darts at the target, hoping to get them right in the middle. The closer you get to the bull's-eye, the more points you receive.

In life, many of us are throwing darts with all our strength, but we're doing it in the dark. We don't even know where the target is. God didn't create us to throw blindly and aimlessly into the future; He created us to find our target and to aim directly at it. He created us to live on purpose. Friend, God created you. He even knows the exact number of hairs on your head! He cares about every aspect of your life. He wants to make the target obvious to you so that you can see and shoot with clear vision.

Right now, I encourage you to ask Him to show you what He sees for every aspect of your life—your career, marriage, family, finances, health, friendships, etc. Write it down. Begin to pray about it. Meditate on it. You'll wake up every day more excited than you were the day before. When a person discovers his or her target and aims with eyes fixed on it, there is much greater precision in the direction life takes.

Now What?

How can we begin to see what God sees, uncover the target for life, and live it out with uncommon vision? There are three ways I recommend.

The first is to go to *God's Word*. Not only will you find the proof that the truths mentioned in this chapter worked for others, but you'll find part of your purpose there too. You'll find promises that God has made for you and uncover part of His vision for your life. As we study the Bible, reading about those who went before us, we will be inspired to live our lives with the same kind of uncommon vision.

Secondly, we should spend time in *God's presence*. The more you know someone, the better you know what he or she would think about a situation. It's the same with God. The more time you spend with Him, the more you start to think, talk, and see as He does.

The final way to live with uncommon vision is by spending time in *God's house*. It's amazing how connecting with like-minded believers can strengthen you. The Bible says that two are better than one, and that is no truer than when we are walking out the purposes God has for us. We are always better together.

When we start to see things the way God does, our vision sparks a deep passion in our hearts that then inspires action, just like it did for me on that stage in the middle of Sierra Leone. Let's look at an example from Mark 6. We see the story of John the Baptist's death. King Herod beheaded him because of John's faith. The Bible says that when Jesus found out about this, He withdrew to a quiet place. He wanted to grieve the loss of His cousin, but upon withdrawing, a great crowd followed Him.

Instead of getting annoyed with the people for not letting Him be alone, or getting frustrated with the disciples for not protecting

Him better, the scripture says that Jesus was moved with compassion. When he *looked* at the multitude of people, deep down inside of Him something erupted—compassion greater than His own challenging situation. Think about that. Jesus' compassion was a direct reflection of what He had *seen*. And that vision produced compassion, which released a passion for holy action. Jesus taught those people all day long, and at the end of the day one of the greatest miracles we know took place—the feeding of the 5,000 which we read about in the last chapter.

Friends, this principle holds just as true in our lives. *When we see what God sees, we will be moved with compassion for others, which produces a passion for His purpose.* Sometimes, we think we've lost the passion for our marriage, family or career, when in reality all we've lost is our vision. If we'll get our vision clear again, our passion will resurface. *Vision always produces passion.*

One of my favorite parts about uncommon vision is that it can be a catalyst for other uncommon traits in our lives—uncommon focus, endurance, and peace. Let's recap. Uncommon vision helped Jesus to have *uncommon focus.* Even in a devastating time, He could focus on what the Father wanted to do. It also helped Him to have *uncommon endurance.* He was tired and weary. He just wanted to get away and rest, but still, He was able to speak all day long. Then, it gave Him *uncommon peace.* In the midst of deep pain, He found comfort in the fact that He was living His purpose. There were people waiting on the other side of His obedience.

So, there's proof that choosing uncommon vision is vital to our walk. *Learning to see the way God sees pushes us farther ahead on our journey than most lessons can.* Maybe there are some things in your life that feel dead or dormant. Maybe you can't see your way out of a tough situation today. I have good news—God can. If you'll choose to adopt His uncommon vision by seeking His

Word, staying in His presence and serving in His House, you'll see the target He wants you to aim for. You will live with an inexplicable focus, endurance and peace even in the midst of adverse circumstances.

I hope you'll decide to let God replace your vision for life with His. I pray that you'll release your perception of how things should be done and accept His. If you'll learn to see through God's eyes, trusting in Him, you'll accomplish more for Him in your lifetime than you could have imagined otherwise.

CHAPTER 7

UNCOMMON PURSUIT

We were living in Hong Kong, and I had just jumped out of a cab with a friend en route to a meeting. Something wasn't right, though. Wallet? Check. Briefcase? Check. Phone? Uh-oh! Where was my phone?! I searched frantically. Then the sickening realization settled on me—the cab. I flung my briefcase to my friend and took off down the road, dodging cars, people, buses, and everything in my way. Just as I was about to reach the car, the light turned green, and it lurched forward. *Maybe I should just give up*, I thought to myself, but I knew that I *needed* my phone. Suddenly, to add to the confusion, two other red taxis pulled in line directly behind the one I was chasing. So now I was running after three red taxis, and I didn't know which one was mine!

I continued running for about three-quarters of a mile. As I got closer, I saw one turn left, one turn right, and one stay straight. *Oh, great.* I thought. *How am I supposed to know which one it is now?* I took a wild guess and kept going straight. The cab slowed to yield to the red stoplight just as I was approaching it. I yelled at the cab driver, and he looked at me, obviously a bit startled. "I need to get my phone. I left it in your car!" I said. After a few seconds, he caught on to what was happening and unlocked the door.

I swung it wide open, fully sweating in my business attire, as the driver continued to watch. I looked around for a few seconds until finally, I saw it. There it was—my precious phone, wedged between the seats. I jumped in and had the driver take me back to where my friend was waiting. I had to pay him twice, but at least I got my phone! It was important to me, so I chased it with everything that I had. It didn't matter what I had to endure.

That's uncommon pursuit. It's the same kind of pursuit we must use for internal and eternal blessings—for chasing God and His purposes. We have to chase so hard that we stop at nothing. When we're pursuing Him fully, we must strive for two things: to know Him and to make Him known.

Know God and Make Him Known

One of the most commonly recited verses in the Bible is Philippians 3:12 (NIV), where Paul wrote, "Not that I have already obtained all this, or have already arrived at my goal, but I press on to take hold of that for which Christ Jesus took hold of me." We like to use this verse to encourage each other to stick it out through difficult times, and to pursue the things God has for us. While that interpretation is good and right, the context of this verse gives it even more meaning. Paul wrote this book to the church in the city of Philippi, while he was in prison for preaching the gospel. Here's a little backstory on Paul: Earlier in his life, he was known for persecuting and killing Christians. As an adult, he had an incredible conversion experience in which He received salvation and surrendered his life to Christ.

From that point on, he lived with an uncommon pursuit of Christ and His Kingdom purpose for his life. He prioritized Him above all else. Even after he knew Christ more intimately than most others, he still wanted more. He wanted to press on and passionately pursue the call of God for his life until he breathed his last breath. I love that he didn't wait until he was perfect to begin his pursuit. The fact is that *in God's eyes, perfection and pursuit have nothing to do with each other.* Regardless of how perfect or imperfect we have been, God wants to know us. He wants us to seek Him with all that we are. And as we seek Him, we will find Him (Jeremiah 29:13).

That's why Paul could literally be sitting in prison as a result of obeying Christ and still love Him with all of his heart. *When we are pursuing God, desiring to know Him above all else, we are able to have peace in the middle of the prison. We are granted a spirit of calmness in the midst of calamity.*

It is what we consistently pursue that we will eventually possess, which is both an encouraging as well as a startling thought. It means that we need to make sure we are pursuing the right things. If we are chasing money, power, fame, etc., we'll end up with something of external value, not eternal value. Likewise, if we focus only on seeking acceptance, we will end up empty. However, when we pursue Jesus, He will give us all of Himself. He will reward us with an abundant life, greater than anything we could ever attempt to create on our own. Matthew 6:33 (NIV) puts it this way: "But seek first his kingdom and his righteousness, and all these things will be given to you as well." Again, what does *all* mean in Greek? Hebrew? English? It means ALL. No matter what way you look at it, no matter what translation you use, all means all. God is always faithful to reward you with ALL He has for you when you put Him first.

God does not want to *take* from our lives; He wants to *add* to them. Others may try to convince us to seek momentary satisfaction, but Jesus gives us proper perspective. When He is put first, He ultimately brings nothing but benefit into our lives. The second step in uncommon pursuit is making God known. That's what happened to Paul, after he began to understand God for who He really was. He couldn't help but share him with others, so he set out on missionary journeys, telling people about the love of Jesus and starting churches in their towns. There are people doing this today, too.

I'll never forget one of my first trips to the Philippines. My driver was a businessman who owned a local dealership. One morning, as we were setting some things up for outreaches later in the day, we stopped at a hotel for lunch. After eating, I went to the bathroom and when I returned I found the businessman talking to someone. I politely waited for him to finish, and when he was done, I asked if he knew the man. "No, I don't," he replied, "But that was the owner of the hotel we just ate at, and he just gave his life to Jesus." How awesome is that? This man wasn't a preacher or an evangelist. He was a businessman with an uncommon pursuit after the things of God. In choosing to live uncommonly, the hotel owner's life was changed forever. And who knows how many other lives will be changed as a result.

We may not all have the same realm of influence, but we *do* all have influence. He has given us each specific families, businesses, workplaces, neighborhoods, etc. He's not looking for us to make the most of what we don't have; that's just impractical. Rather, He wants us to make the most of what we *do* have, to pour our lives into knowing Him and making Him known in our worlds. Knowing God is not about reading your Bible a few days out of the week and attending church every Sunday. It's about pursuing a relationship with the Father no matter the cost.

Making God known is not about a specific job. It's not about being called to the ministry. In John 17:18 (ESV), Jesus says to the

Father, "Just as you sent me into the world, I am sending them into the world." That means He is sending us into every field, career, and part of the world to declare His goodness. My takeaway from this verse is simple: *Own your story, and watch what God will do.*

I love the old Clint Eastwood movie clips when he would pull out his gun and say confidently, "I'll make you famous." That's what I want. I want to be serious about making Jesus famous. When people look at my family, my marriage, my friendships, my health, and my finances. I want those things to speak volumes about the God I serve. Don't you?

Live With the End in Mind

Do you ever think about the end of your life? How many people will gather to celebrate it and what they will say? I do, not to be morbid but because it helps me put the days I have left on earth into perspective. We will all be remembered in some way, and we all have a deep longing for it to be a way that matters. As we start out on this path of pursuit, we will certainly be met with seasons of discouragement. During those times, there's a way of thinking that always helps me to pull through: living with the end in mind.

I was reminded of this truth when I attended my uncle's funeral. I was close to him growing up, but the older I got, the less I saw him and the less I knew of his life. I was aware that he was successful and had a lot of friends, but that is about it. When I arrived at the funeral home, I was shocked at what I saw. There were hundreds of people in a line formed all the way outside and around the home. They neither looked the same, nor did they all seem to be in the same line of work. None of that mattered as they celebrated how this man had touched their lives.

Inside the home, I saw everyone from the mayor of his city to a group of once-homeless men that my uncle had helped. My favorite part of the service was when his son, my cousin, got up and shared about his father. He talked about how genuine he was, about how he acted the same to the person begging on the street as he did to the banker behind a desk. "I think the reason he was so genuine is because he had a genuine relationship with Christ," he explained. He then described how my uncle would get up early in the morning and go to the only empty space in the house that he could find—the garage—and pray. There he would talk to His Father and spend time with Him. My cousin strongly believed that knowing God in this intimate way is what changed not only my uncle's life, but also every person that he came into contact with. It's what had affected the life of every person in that room.

It was obvious that my uncle had lived a life different than most—a life marked by uncommon pursuit. Anyone can pursue things just enough to get by, but we are called to much more. So right now, think about your life. Think about the end of it. What do you want people to say about you? Do you want an average amount of people gathered, celebrating an average life of an average man or woman? I don't. I want to be in constant uncommon pursuit of God. I want to make an uncommon impact because of how I uncommonly pursued a relationship with my Heavenly Father.

On the Right Track

How do you know you are on the right track in your pursuit of God? Let me tell you a story that I believe will help you grasp this idea better. A few years ago, my family was flying back from Asia where we were doing mission work. It was a 26-hour flight, and we had our two children with us—Isaac, who was four years old at the time and Lizzie, who was two years old.

As we deplaned, we groggily headed toward the baggage claim. As most parents know, traveling with two small kids is intense! You have so much to keep track of—strollers, car seats, bottles, diapers, and the list goes on. So we gathered our overwhelming number of items and headed off to the side of the baggage claim area to regroup. It wasn't until I started talking to them that I realized something—Isaac wasn't with us! In the middle of the Tokyo airport, my son was lost. I looked panicked at my wife and then without saying anything, I took off. I ran around the airport, hurriedly searching in a sea of Asian people for a little blond boy.

I ran up to several people asking them if they'd seen him, fully knowing they didn't speak my language. I knocked things over. I ran into things. I even pushed people! I did whatever I had to, until finally, around the corner, I saw little Isaac. I ran up to him, and he just smiled and gave me a big hug. Despite my relief, I couldn't help but think, *You little stinker! Do you know the panic you've caused me?* On the way back to my wife and daughter I realized how crazy I must've looked. Then I had an even greater realization—I didn't care! What I was pursuing was so much more important than how I was perceived by those around me.

As we close this chapter, I challenge you to take inventory of your life. Are you living with uncommon pursuit, or are you simply waiting for God's blessing to come to you? *When we pursue God no matter how crazy we look to those around us, that's when we're living with uncommon pursuit.* When we, like Paul, press toward God with everything that we have in a desire to know Him and make Him known, we will be rewarded for our faithfulness.

CHAPTER 8

UNCOMMON FAITH

I may not know you personally, but I do know something about you, and you may get a little upset when I tell you what it is. Still want to know? Alright. Here it is. You're not good enough. You're not good enough now, and you never will be.

Caleb, how dare you!

I can almost feel your offense through the pages! And I understand why you feel that way. Almost every self-help book has told you differently. You might think I'm being harsh, but it would be harsher for me to let you think otherwise. Still upset? Please bear with me a little longer because I actually want to help you out right now. Here's what I mean: *It's only when we realize that we aren't good enough, that we can accept that God is.* And it's only when we accept God's goodness that He can work on our behalf like He wants to. It's only then that He can move us beyond our limitations.

The Bible is filled with people who surrendered their ego in order to be a part of God's bigger story. Moses is a great example. He knew he wasn't good enough to lead the people of Israel out of slavery. He was a murderer! Plus, he could hardly utter a sentence without stuttering. God didn't call Moses because he was good enough; He called Moses because he was willing to fully rely on his Heavenly Father. What about David? He was the youngest son in a family of shepherds, the lowliest profession of that day. Was he good enough to be the greatest king of Israel? Not without God. What about Rahab, the prostitute? Or Esther, the orphan? *God isn't just looking for someone who is "good." He's looking for someone who will let Him be.*

This point is proven perfectly in the battle plan that God gave Gideon in Judges 7. As Gideon was about to lead his men into battle against the Midianites, God said, "You have too many men. I cannot deliver Midian into their hands, or Israel would boast against me, saying, 'My own strength has saved me.'" So, God separated Gideon's soldiers. First, He told Gideon to announce to the army, "Anyone who is afraid may go home." 22,000 men left immediately. Only 10,000 remained.

Amazingly, God told Gideon there were *still* too many. He then instructed him to have the men get water to drink. Gideon obeyed. God told him to keep the ones who lapped up the water from cupped hands and to send away those who knelt down to lap directly from the stream. Only 300 remained. In one day, Gideon's army went from 32,000 to 300. Do you think they felt good enough? Absolutely not! But that's right where God wanted them. He wanted them to rely on His strength—not their own. They did, and it caused them to win the battle against Midian in epic fashion.

You Have What it Takes

So now that we've all accepted the fact that we're not good enough, I want you to know something else. You have what it takes.

What? That makes no sense! You just told me I wasn't good enough!

Again, I can feel your frustration, so let me explain. You have what it takes not because of your skills, abilities or education, but because you have Jesus living inside of you. As a believer in Christ, you have everything you need to carry out God's purposes for your life. It's just like when God spoke to me after I preached my first message in Ghana. You have what it takes because you have His Son inside of you. And that's all you need.

Let's return to Gideon again, because his backstory, told in Judges 6, is one that proves this point well. First of all, Gideon literally means "He that cuts down." Doesn't sound like someone you want around, does it? He came from an undistinguished family and had little training in the area of leadership and combat. Furthermore, when God called him, he was threshing wheat in a winepress. You don't thresh wheat in a winepress.

Suddenly, an angel appeared to him, and the angel's first words were, "The Lord is with you, mighty warrior." Then, the angel told him to lead the fight against the Midianites. Gideon's initial response was less than faith-filled. "Pardon me, my lord," he replied. "But how can I save Israel? My clan is the least in Manasseh, and I am the least in my family!" God responded, and His answer echoed what the angel had said, "I will be with you."

In other words, when Gideon said, "I'm not good enough," God responded, "You have what it takes." Gideon still had major doubts, but God reassured him of both His presence as well as His call on Gideon's life. Day after day, Gideon's faith was strengthened until he eventually led the Israelites to victory. I think that many of us can identify with Gideon. We know God has a call on our lives, but we don't feel good enough to live it out. The turning point comes when we recognize that we have what it takes because we have Jesus living inside us. Just like Gideon, when we live with faith in God, He will always lead us into great victory.

Joshua's story was similar. He didn't feel worthy to lead the Israelites into the Promised Land—especially after Moses had led them for years! Yet, he also knew that God had called him. All throughout his journey, God encouraged him (like in Deuteronomy 31:6, NIV) over and over again: "Be strong and very courageous. I will be with you wherever you go." Joshua knew he wasn't good enough, but he also lived in the reality of God's presence in his life. He had a Father who was leading him, so he walked with confidence, leading the Israelites into the Promised Land.

Both of these men showed uncommon faith in God, trusting that they had what it took, though they themselves weren't good enough. And that faith is what made all the difference, not only in their lives but also in each life that they interacted with.

Who's Your Coach?

Every person I've mentioned so far had faith that he or she would experience victory because someone else did first. That's usually the way it goes. We doubt our abilities to act with great faith until someone calls it out in us.

I learned this in high school while playing in a summer league basketball game. We were down four points, and only 15 seconds remained in the game. My teammate threw the ball to me. I dribbled down the side of the court toward the basket to score. As I released the ball, I was fouled. As I walked to the free-throw line to take my shots, I looked at the game clock. There were only five seconds left. *There's no way,* I thought. *The game is over. Even if I make both of these, we're still down two.*

As I'm thinking these things to myself, I hear the whistle blow. My coach had called a timeout, so I ran to the huddle, feeling discouraged. I was surprised at Coach's enthusiasm. "Okay, here's what's going to happen," he said. "You're going to make the first shot." *Okay? That's the big plan?* I wondered, but he continued, "Then, on the second shot, you're going to miss it." *Yep, he's crazy,* I concluded. He continued, "Throw it off the front of the rim so that the ball bounces right back to you. Get it, head over to the three-point line and take a shot before time expires. I believe you're going to make that shot, and we'll win the game."

My teammates and I stared blankly at each other for a few seconds. Thoughts were flooding my mind like, *Have you noticed how skinny the rim is? How am I supposed to shoot it that perfectly? Do you realize that there are a bunch of other guys lined up for the rebound? How do I get it to come directly to me?* I voiced some of these concerns in the few seconds we had left. He stopped me mid-sentence, looked at me sternly and said, "You're going to do it, Caleb. I have coached you all season. I know that you have what it takes."

My faith wasn't at the level of my coach's, but those words sparked something in me. *You have what it takes, Caleb,* I kept telling myself as I walked back up to the line. *Okay, here we go,* I thought. I pulled up and released the first shot. Swoosh. I looked back at Coach. He nodded and smiled. I released the second shot. It bounced off the rim directly to me. I grabbed it, dribbled to the three-point line and released it again. The buzzer went off as we all held our breath. The ball bounced once...twice...three times... and then...unbelievably it went in! I could hardly believe it, and neither could my teammates. We went into overtime and ended up winning the game. We celebrated big that day, and I realized that I really did have what it took. I just needed someone to call it out in me.

Friends, that's who God wants to be to us. He wants to be our coach, calling things out of us that we never would have seen on our own. He wants to lead us into greater victories than we ever thought possible, but we must learn to listen as well as to believe what He says. Then we've got to have the courage to take the shot.

It's a Heart Matter

Several years ago, I developed a friendship with a brother from an extremely impoverished third-world country. His dream had always been to move to America, graduate from a well-known Christian university, and take what he learned back to his country to minister to his people. There were just two problems. First, he knew no one in the United States. Second, he had no money. None.

So, he began saving. After a long time, he accumulated enough to buy a one-way plane ticket to the States. He applied to the university and got accepted. He took the step to go, still having no money for school and no contacts once he got there. He registered for classes and got into all of the ones he wanted, but then, it was time to pay for them. He told me that up until this point, it was easier to have faith because he could control some aspect of the situation. He worked hard to save the money for his ticket, and he worked hard to get accepted. The payment situation, however, was out of his control. There was nothing he could do but have uncommon faith that God would help him. So, that's what he did.

My friend stood in the admissions line, praying. He tallied up how much money he would need to make it through the semester and whispered that number in prayer. "God, I don't know how you're going to do this, but I know that you will. I have faith in your willingness and ability to fulfill your promises to me," he whispered. Every once in a while, his thoughts would start to waver. *Hey, did you forget? You have no money! You're about to be embarrassed in front of everyone!*

Yet, his heart kept believing that somehow God was going to do the impossible. Person-by-person, my friend moved closer to the front of the line. Finally, there was only one person left in front of him. My friend continued to fight the battle raging between his head and his heart, when suddenly he felt a tap on his shoulder. He turned around to a stranger handing him an envelope. *What is this?* He wondered. He thanked the stranger, took the envelope and looked around. To his surprise, no one else had received an envelope.

Do they know that I don't have enough money? Are they asking me to leave before I get embarrassed? Doubt continued to bombard his mind. He reluctantly opened the envelope. Inside, there was no note, just a stack of crisp one hundred dollar bills. He counted them. Sure enough, it was the exact amount to pay for his classes—in cash. How incredible is that? What's even better about this story is that such things didn't just happen one semester, but every single semester my friend was in school. He was able to pay his bills, finish his courses, and go back to his country, not just with his undergraduate degree, but also with his master's and doctorate degrees! They were all paid for supernaturally because he chose to operate in uncommon faith and believe even when it seemed impossible.

That's the kind of road we're all called to walk as believers. That's the kind of blessing we're meant to experience. Like my friend we'll have times we can't make sense of things. We'll have moments when our heads battle with our hearts. In those times, we have to keep choosing our hearts. *The enemy can attack our minds, but he can't touch our hearts.* As we live with uncommon faith in God's promises, we'll find that though we aren't good enough, we still have what it takes. *Because we have a faithful Father, we can win the battle of heart over head.* We can walk in triumph experiencing all the beautiful things God has planned for us.

Know Your Weapons

There are two main weapons that you'll need in the battle to keep your faith strong: perseverance and praise. Hebrews 10:35-36 (NIV) gives us the connection between perseverance and faith: "So do not throw away your confidence; it will be richly rewarded. You need to persevere so that when you have done the will of God, you will receive what he has promised." On the road to victory, we will have to choose to get back up time and time again, no matter how hard the fall. Then, we'll have to choose to praise God, even when things look like they're not getting any better.

Sarah and I put both of these into practice on our first trip to Asia as a family. We felt we had already exhibited big faith by choosing to go; we didn't realize that faith isn't a one-time decision. On the flight, the unthinkable happened. Our infant son Isaac stopped breathing. The medical team resuscitated him and put him on oxygen, but then he began to experience powerful seizures. As soon as we landed, we rushed to several hospitals seeking immediate help for his physical condition.

Truthfully, the more we pondered the situation, the more doubt flooded our minds. *What kind of parents are we, bringing our kids to the other side of the world? Did we really hear God? Maybe we should just turn around.* Those thoughts plagued us incessantly, but we chose to keep going. One night, as we were fighting doubt and condemnation, Sarah told me, "Caleb, it's good that we keep persevering, but we also need to praise. We need to act like we've already been given the victory." She then worshiped like I've never seen her worship before. She shifted her focus from her situation to her Solution, confessing that our hope is solely in our Heavenly Father.

Of course, I joined in, and as we praised, God began to download to us how we were to take care of Isaac. We obeyed His instructions, and Isaac has never suffered another seizure since that day. How great is our God? When we operate in uncommon faith, persevering through each trial and praising through each doubt, He always gives us the victory. I charge you today to approach whatever situation you're in with that same uncommon faith—the kind that makes people look at you and think *Are they crazy?* I promise you, God notices when we operate in uncommon faith.

CHAPTER 9

UNCOMMON LOVE

I think the word *love* might just be the most overused word in the English language. We love the cake we ate for dessert last night. We love our spouse. We love our favorite football team. We love our kids. We love our morning coffee. And we love Jesus. Do you see what I'm saying? "Love" is used so often and so broadly that it's meaning has been diluted. It doesn't mean much anymore. In our generation it's become a weak word, not just in speech, but many times, in action as well. While the world around us demonstrates hollow love, as believers, we're called to love differently. We're called to love—you guessed it—uncommonly.

On one of my recent trips to Cambodia, we held an outreach in one of our children's homes. We had just finished giving out Christmas presents and were leaving, when I felt the Lord speak to my spirit. He told me to look out the vehicle's back window. I wasn't expecting what happened next. As I looked at the groups of children with huge smiles on their faces, I became so overwhelmed with emotion that I began to weep.

They say sometimes you understand things in a moment. And that day, in that moment, I believe I truly "understood" uncommon love. When we allow the love of our Father to work through us, it brings our hearts immeasurable joy and satisfaction. I think it goes without saying that the best demonstration of uncommon love is Jesus himself. He proved this not only through His death, the most sacrificial demonstration of love, but also through His life.

Scripture is filled with stories of Jesus' love. It's obvious in story after story that He doesn't discriminate between people or groups. He loves everyone the same. Two of my favorite examples of this are found in Mark 10. First, Jesus showed His love by extending it to everyone, even the children, who could offer Him no physical gift in return. Verse 13 tells us that when people brought their kids to Jesus to pray for them, the disciples rebuked them.

When Jesus realized what His disciples were doing, He was indignant. That's where the famous passage is found: "Let the little children come to me, and do not hinder them, for the kingdom of God belongs to such as these. Truly I tell you, anyone who will not receive the kingdom of God like a little child will never enter it." The fact that Jesus loves children, who can offer nothing in return, proves the genuineness of His love. He truly loves everyone, without condition. He doesn't give to get. *He just gives to give.*

The second story is found at the end of this same chapter. Verse 46 introduces a blind man named Bartimaeus who screamed out, "Jesus, have mercy on me!" as He passed by. People all around him urged him to quiet down, but Jesus heard his cry and stopped. He asked for the disciples to bring the man to Him, and that day the man's blindness was healed. Jesus exhibited true love to Bartimaeus when no one else would. That's love in its truest form. In Romans 5:8 (NKJV), Jesus tells us, "I loved you at your darkest." He loves us with an uncommon love, each and every day. And He tells us in John 15:12 that we are called to love one another just as He has loved us.

Everyone Matters

My wife often tells the story about a young boy walking along the beach who noticed thousands of starfish that had washed up on shore. He knew they wouldn't live without water, so he began to pick them up one by one and throw them back in. As he did, an older man spotted him. He watched for a while before approaching. "Hey, son, what are you doing?" he asked. "I'm saving the starfish!" the little boy replied with an urgent tone. "If I don't throw them in, they'll die!"

The old man replied, "But there are miles of beach and thousands of starfish. What makes you think this is really making a difference?" The boy looked at him with a bit of naïve confusion. Then he picked one up, and said, "It makes a difference to this one...and this one...and this one...." The man was stunned by the boy's compassion. He couldn't speak, so he joined the boy, picking up the starfish one by one. That's how uncommon love thinks. *It's not just about loving large masses of people. It's about loving the ONE in front of you.*

Jesus was great at focusing on the one. We see story after story of Him choosing to go out of His way for just one person. For example, He sailed through the storm to find the one man who was in dire need of deliverance. In Mark 5, Jesus had just finished teaching multitudes of people. He was exhausted, I'm sure. But He knew that someone needed His uncommon love. So, He chose to get in a boat and sail to the region of the Gerasenes. On the way, He and His disciples encountered a great storm.

The disciples were afraid and wanted to turn around, but Jesus knew there was a man who needed Him desperately. So He calmed the waves, rested as much as He could on the journey, and arrived in the region of the Gerasenes. The man Jesus sailed for had been excommunicated from his community because he was demon-possessed. Scripture describes him as being a danger to himself and to those around him, but Jesus cared about this man's soul more than He cared about His own comfort. He cast the demons out of that man and changed his life forever.

Another great example of Jesus going out of His way for one person is the story of the woman at the well in Samaria. Let me give you a little bit of context: Samaria was between Galilee in the north and Judea and Jerusalem in the south. The shortest way to get from one to the other was to go through Samaria. However, Samaritans and Jews had been enemies for hundreds of years due to religious differences, so Jews would typically go the long way *around* Samara in order to reach their destination. It had been this way for years—going *through* Samaria wasn't a viable option.

Yet we know that Jesus specialized in doing things differently. His forte is living in the uncommon. He knew there was a woman in Samaria who needed to know His love. So, He went against the status quo, and He traveled straight through Samaria. In John 4 we read that Jesus talked to the woman. He even asked her to pour him some water, shocking her greatly. If Jews refused to even speak to Samaritans, they certainly wouldn't drink from the same cup, right? Wrong. *Jesus' love breaks the religious rules because it's daring, brave and constant.*

That woman's life was totally changed that day as she experienced for the first time a love she had spent her whole life searching for. John tells us that she had been married five times and when Jesus found her, she was living with a man she was not married to. She had been in relationships with men with a common love, a conditional love. By contrast, when she met Jesus, He showed her what real love is—unconditional and uncommon.

Who might be the Samaritan woman in your life? Who might you have to sail through the storm for? When we choose to go out of our way, to love without limits, we become more and more like Jesus. We become uncommon.

Love Fully

As children of God, we are the greatest conduits of His love. When we love well, people can feel how Jesus feels about them. We are called not only to show this love by going out of our way to love every person, but we are also called to love every person fully.

This truth is a game changer. When we know the full love of Jesus, we can exhibit it fully in the lives of others. In Ephesians 3:17-21 (NIV), Paul explains this idea when he says, 'I pray that you, being rooted and established in love, may have power, together with all the saints, to grasp how wide and long and high and deep is the love of Christ, and to know this love that surpasses knowledge—that you may be filled to the measure of all the fullness of God. Now to him who is able to do immeasurably more than all we ask or imagine, according to His power that is at work within us....'

Paul is basically saying that when we know God's love fully, it will blow our minds. It'll leave us in awe of His goodness and spark in us a passion to show others this same type of uncommon love. Paul goes on to explain the four aspects of God's love

The first is the *wide* love of Jesus—the love that reaches far. This is the love that can find us, no matter how far we've run. Next Paul talks about Christ's *long* love. That is the aspect of love that changes us. It works on us and walks with us, maturing us into all we are meant to become. Third, Paul mentions God's *high* love. This love pushes us higher and into greater blessing than we ever thought we could experience in our lifetimes. Finally, he touches on God's deep love. This is the one that reaches down into any pit we've fallen into and pulls us out. As Isaiah 59:1 (NIV) says, "The arm of the Lord is not too short to save, nor his ear too dull to hear."

That passage in Ephesians gives us the perfect instruction on how to love fully. Love wide, reaching out to everyone, no matter how lost, marginalized, sick, or sinful. Love long. Walk with people on their road to salvation and healing. Help them to develop their full potential. Then, love high. Teach them about God's blessings and help them to reach for them. Finally, love deep. Reach into the depths of their hearts, and pull them out of the pit they've lost themselves in. And don't be afraid of getting dirty. Sometimes, that's what love takes.

Give to Give

One of the best ways to know you love uncommonly is that you give love even when you don't receive it in return. Again, let's take a look at our perfect example. Jesus loved even when those He loved most betrayed him. For example, He loved Peter, even when Peter denied knowing Him at all. This disloyalty came after three years of intimate friendship—three years of watching Jesus' love impact multitudes and somehow personally transform his own life.

Following Peter's denial, Jesus had been crucified and resurrected. Going to the shore of the lake He saw his disciples in their boats, discouraged after fishing all night and catching nothing. Jesus called out to them, telling them to throw their nets on the other side. Though they could hardly see Him and didn't know who He was, they listened. When they did, they pulled in more fish than their nets could carry. In that moment, John, one of the disciples, recognized that this was Jesus. When he shared this insight with Peter, Peter jumped into the water and headed toward His Savior. As he approached, I'm sure Peter was replaying the denial in his mind. I'm sure he was plagued by insurmountable guilt and shame.

When Peter arrived at the shore, Jesus didn't condemn him, though He could have. He simply said, "Bring some of the fish you have caught." Then, Jesus started making breakfast. After they finished eating, Jesus addressed Peter directly. He asked a pointed question, "Peter, do you love me?" Peter responded, "Lord, you know that I love you." Jesus responded, "Then feed my lambs." (Jesus was calling Peter to lead the early church.)

Jesus repeated this same question and received the same answer two more times. I believe He did it once for each of Peter's denials. He wanted to prove that His love was big enough to cover any and every mistake. Friends, *this* is uncommon love.

Another great example of this unconditional devotion is found in the story of Hosea. Let me ask you something. If God gave you direction to marry someone you knew would be unfaithful, would you marry him or her? It would be pretty tough, right? That's what happened to Hosea. God asked him to marry a prostitute, informing him ahead of time that she would be unfaithful. Now, if you're looking for a mate, don't use this story as advice. I highly doubt God wants that for you. So what is the point of the story? At this point in history, God needed a dramatic example to prove His redemptive love to the people of Israel.

Hosea married Gomer, and they had three children. One day Gomer decided she didn't want the responsibility of being a wife and mother anymore. So, she left Hosea and returned to her old ways. Hosea was heartbroken, but he continued to raise his three children, teaching them the ways of God. After a while, the Lord spoke to Hosea about Gomer. He told him to go find her, and then pay whatever price it would take to get her back. Amazingly, Hosea brought her home and continued to love her and take care of her the rest of her life.

I don't know how you'd feel, but that would be pretty tough for me. After all, she *chose* to leave! Nevertheless, Hosea was obedient. He exhibited God's consistent love to Gomer. He rescued his wife from her troubles and loved her well, even when she didn't reciprocate. That's how God is with us. *Even when we are unfaithful with our love, He is faithful.* Human love may fail, but as 1 Corinthians 13:8 (NIV) says, God's "love never fails." It's not common to be kind to people who are unkind to you. It's not common to love when you receive nothing in return. Remember, though, that we aren't called to be common.

Love Today

Now that we've defined uncommon love and shown the incredible effect it can have on a life, I'm sure you're ready to demonstrate it. Sometimes, though, it can seem a little daunting to know where to start, right? How do we love *today*?

The first thing for us to remember is simply to *love the one in front of us*. We don't have to travel to the ends of the earth to show love. We can start with our spouse, our kids, our boss, our friends and our co-workers.

Next, we have to just do it. We must *put our compassion into action* because love doesn't just sit around. Uncommon love gets out there and does something. Living this way truly changes your life. When you start loving uncommonly, interruptions start looking a whole lot more like divine appointments. Random run-ins start looking a whole lot like strategic setups.

The beautiful bottom line is this: *Heaven can invade earth through your uncommon love.* As you seek to love as Jesus did, heaven will change people through you. So, I encourage you today to go out of your way to love dangerously. Love people who don't deserve it. Love fully, meeting people right where they are, but loving them too much to let them stay there. And give them love always, even when you don't get anything back. God's mandate to us is simple—love all people, all the time. Will you accept it? If you'll make His mandate your life's mission, He will work through you in uncommon ways.

CHAPTER 10

UNCOMMON PEACE

On my way to Asia several years ago, my airline ticket revealed the terrible news that anyone with my kind of height dreads—I would be sitting at the rear of the plane in a middle seat. This was going to be a 15-hour flight, so I wasn't thrilled about it. Since I arrived early, I approached the attendant behind the desk to inquire about other options.

"Sir, are there any other seats available?" I asked politely, but hopefully. He just glanced at me for a moment and then went right back to his computer. "I'll see what I can do," he finally muttered with his eyes still avoiding contact with mine. About 30 minutes later, they called us to board. I walked up to the desk to discover my fate. Again, barely looking at me, the man handed me my new ticket with a simple, "Have a nice flight."

I tried not to look at the document too quickly. Finally, though, I couldn't resist—*7A. Yes! This is not my same seat*, I thought. I was thrilled, but then I thought about it a little more. *7A? I've never seen that small of a number on a boarding pass before. I don't even know where that is.* I followed the cabin numbers to my seat. Of course, as you probably realize by now, it was a first-class seat. I had been upgraded! I thanked God for that attendant right then and there. The entire flight, I had all the legroom I needed, I was able to recline, take some good naps, and even eat as much food as I wanted with no additional cost! It was a much-welcomed surprise. The truth is that we all like upgrades, don't we? Not just on flights, or with cars and phones, but upgrades in life as well.

I have discovered that God wants to upgrade every area of our lives. He wants us to live as overcomers. He doesn't want us to succumb to our circumstances but to walk in victory each and every day. He wants to upgrade us outwardly, but to do that, we first have to be upgraded inwardly. One of the best ways He upgrades us internally is by giving us His peace to rule our hearts. It's a free gift, but we do have to choose it. Every time we face something that would agitate us or cause anxiety, we have to choose peace.

Colossians 3:15 (NLT) says, "And let the peace that comes from Christ rule in your hearts. For as members of one body you are called to live in peace." Another version—God's Word translation—literally says, "Let Christ's peace control you." When we learn to live guided by the peace of God, absolutely nothing will be able to divert us from His purpose. Nothing! That's a pretty good upgrade, if you ask me. Philippians 4:7 (NLT) gives more insight into how God's peace enriches our lives. It says, "Then you will experience God's peace, which exceeds anything we can understand. His peace will guard your hearts and minds as you live in Christ Jesus."

This means that we can have a calm spirit, even when circumstances don't make sense. In the middle of the storm, we can be still and calm. When we should be running around frantically, we can stop, listen and respond to His voice in faith. No matter the uncertainty we find ourselves in, it's His peace that passes all understanding that can rule in our hearts and minds. Provided we choose His peace, we can have our hearts and minds protected from even the fiercest of storms.

God is Greater

When I was a kid, my dad used to give me outside chores to do around the house. One day, he instructed me to attach a trailer in our backyard to his truck. Initially, I thought it would be an easy task, but I overestimated my abilities quite a bit. I tried several times before asking my brother for help. Together we couldn't get it attached either! We kept trying, but we just weren't strong enough. After a while, Dad walked out and saw the trailer still sitting in the same place it had been before. He asked, "What is my trailer doing still sitting there?"

Our heads dropped a little, as we realized we'd have to drop our egos and admit our weakness. "We can't get it, Dad. It's too heavy," I explained. We waited for a scolding, but he just smiled a little and then walked over to the trailer. Incredibly, he lifted that thing up with what seemed like one finger and hooked it to the truck with ease. I'm pretty sure I was convinced my dad was a superhero after that. I walked around telling my school friends how strong he was and how he could do anything.

Fast forward to a tough situation I went through a few years ago. I was extremely discouraged, praying about what to do. Suddenly, God reminded me of my dad lifting that trailer that had seemed so heavy to my brother and me. After witnessing my dad's strength, I had such a simple faith that he could do anything. If I trusted my earthly father to handle life's burdens with ease, why couldn't I trust my Heavenly Father? After all, He knows *no* earthly limits. This thought brought immediate peace to my heart that day, and it still does.

Friends, it doesn't matter what you're facing today; *nothing is too big for God.* I believe that it's time for us to rise up in faith and understand the true strength of our Father. *He is bigger than anything we could ever face. His love swallows the situations we think we're drowning in.* John 16:33 (NIV) says, "I have told you these things, so that in me you may have peace. In this world you will have trouble. But take heart! I have overcome the world."

God gives us peace, not just to help us feel calm everyday, but He also gives us a deep-rooted peace for the real challenges of life. Apply it that sickness you can't see yourself being healed from, the marriage you can't see coming together, and the child you can't see returning to the Lord. We know that God is greater than any circumstance, trouble, and trial—no matter how heavy it may seem.

It may feel like your current battle is too hard, but take heart: God has already won the war. Right now, I want you to do a little homework. Grab a piece of paper and write down every challenge, trial, or issue going on in your life. What has caused you stress, or made you feel confused? Where is fear entering your heart? It doesn't matter how big or how small your situation seems to you. If it concerns you, it concerns God. Don't hold anything back because He already knows.

Now, next to each one I want you to write the words *"...BUT God is greater."* Next I want you to read them out loud and do so every time you start to worry. As soon as you start to feel confusion taking over your heart, invite God's peace in. When we realize the greatness of our God, we begin to see our life, our future, and our entire world differently. This is what choosing to allow His peace to control us is all about. We *can* take heart, for our victory has already been won.

Through the Fire

One of the greatest examples of uncommon peace is found in the story of Shadrach, Meshach, and Abednego in Daniel 3. I'll paraphrase it. These three Hebrew boys were Daniel's hometown friends. They grew up believing in the same God before being deported to Babylon by Israel's archenemy, Babylon. One day, the king of Babylon, Nebuchadnezzar, issued a decree. It stated that when a certain song was played throughout the land, everyone had to bow to a statue of the king to show him honor. Such a practice violated their faith in the One True God. They knew they could never bow to this ornate idol, so they told the king that they wouldn't do it.

His response was simple, "You'll bow, or you'll burn." Now let's be honest. Would you agree with me that this would be a completely understandable moment to lose their peace? The king was telling them that they would be thrown into a fiery furnace. Yet they didn't waver. They allowed God's uncommon peace to control their hearts. Their response to the king demonstrated their confidence in their Father's strength. "Oh, king," they answered. "We have no need to answer you in this matter. If you do throw us in the fire, our God will deliver us from your hands. But if not, let it be known, oh, king, that we will not worship any idols."

They chose to honor God in the midst of criticism and compromise. And when we honor God, He always honors us. The king did as he said. He had his attendants throw all three boys into the fire. And not only that, but he had the fire turned up seven times hotter than normal. It was so intense that the soldiers who threw them in the furnace were immediately killed! The Bible says that after a couple of minutes, the king leapt to his feet in amazement. "Didn't we tie up three men and throw them into the blazing furnace?" he asked. "Yes, we did, Your Majesty." They answered. "Then why do I see four men walking around in the fire? They are not tied up, and they show no sign of being hurt—and the fourth one looks like an angel."

Shadrach, Meshach and Abednego sought God's peace in the midst of their trouble, and He showed up in the flames with them. The king then called them to come out of the fire. All of the princes, governors, lieutenant governors, and other officials gathered in shock to look at the three men. They had not been harmed in any way by the fire. Their hair was not singed, their clothes were not burned, and there was no smell of smoke on them. That day, the king's heart was changed. He passed a law that if anyone spoke against the God of Shadrach, Meshach, and Abednego, he would die. An entire nation experienced the glory of God. And it all happened because three political refugees recognized that God was greater than their trouble. When they faced *pressure* with peace, they experienced God's *power* leading to *promotion* in their lives.

It's the same with us. When we are in a place of pressure, we can choose peace. When we do so, God's power is made available to us, and we are promoted (or upgraded) into the life He has for us. In my experience, this peace usually upgrades our lives in three main areas: *confidence, clarity* and *courage*.

Confidence: When I read the story of Shadrach, Meshach, and Abednego, I sometimes think about what the fiery furnace must have been like for them. I mean it's just a story to us. It was their *bodies* that were almost roasted alive. I am sure they had questions like, "God why are we about to be thrown into this fire for doing what you want? We've done nothing but be obedient!" I'm sure they had to overcome doubt more than a few times. They needed uncommon confidence that is the result of God's peace in the midst of pressure.

Confidence deals with a mindset, behavior or attitude that you have about your situation that others don't have. If someone else had been in these guys' position, he may not have had the same response. In choosing to let God's peace control their hearts and minds, God saw fit for their story to become part of our Scriptures. The truth is this: *Whatever you have confidence in will be the first thing you run to when pressure is applied.*

Do you have confidence in your work ethic? In your money? In your family and friends? In your psychiatrist, doctor, or medicine? Or is your confidence in God? I'm not saying that people and things can't help us through problems, because they can, and God often uses them for that purpose. God is the only one, however, who can give us *complete* victory.

When my wife and I were youth pastors, we took a group of junior high students to Mexico. As we were ministering in one village, a few of the students decided to enter a shack to pray for the people living there. Inside, they found a woman who was blind in both eyes. These teenagers had heard us talk about how God could do miracles, and they decided to see if it was true. Without wasting time they went straight up to her, asked her if they could pray for her, and went into full intercession mode. They weren't playing! They called down Heaven in that room.

After a few minutes, the woman started yelling in Spanish. Sure enough, our translator told us that she had been healed. The kids' confidence skyrocketed. From that point on, they would stop and pray for anything or anyone without hesitation. Miracles happened left and right on that trip. With each one, the students became even bolder than the time before. If you even *tried* to tell them that God was not greater than the issue standing before them, they simply wouldn't listen. In fact, they would have attempted to convince you otherwise because they saw what happened when they chose to walk in the peace that passes all understanding. They saw the problem, but they looked past it to the truth that God is greater. In doing so God upgraded their confidence.

What do you see when you look at your circumstances? The problem or the possibility? Sometimes, God waits until the last possible moment, but He *always* comes through. Don't settle for defeat when God wants you to experience victory. Luke 1:37 tells us that with God, *nothing* will be impossible for us. Nothing. That's because our Father can turn our impossible into possible. It's not even hard for Him. At this point in my life, I accept uncertainty with excitement, because I know that with God uncertainty is nothing more than a blank slate reminding me that anything is still possible.

Clarity: I love the story of Elisha and his servant in 2 Kings 6. In this passage Elisha is fighting against the Syrian army. One morning, his servant reports to him that there are thousands of soldiers with horses and chariots surrounding the town. "We're doomed! What will we do?" the servant asked. Elisha's response is breathtaking. Verses 16-17 give us the account. "Don't be afraid," Elisha answered. "We have more on our side than they have on theirs." Then he prayed, "O Lord, open his eyes and let him see!"

The Lord answered his prayer, and Elisha's servant looked and saw the hillside around the city covered with heaven's fiery horses and chariots. When the servant's eyes were opened, he had a new-found clarity about what God could do. He saw an army of angels stationed around them to fight their battle. He saw that God was on their side, and he realized that God is *always* greater!

Peace deals with our outlook—the way we see things. It narrows our vision so that we focus on what God wants us to see. When God gives you this clarity you begin to see what is *for* you more than what is *against* you. You begin to see what you *have* more than what you *lack*. You begin to see the *favor* and *mercy* of God more than the *negative* emotions and situations that you're experiencing. *God's peace always helps you to see the possibility more than the problem.* When you feel overwhelmed, know that God sees you as an overcomer. He's always fighting with you. So, reset your focus and remember: *There are more with you than there are with them.*

Courage: The final part of this peace promotion is the courage to do things that others are not willing to do. God upgraded Shadrach, Meshach, and Abednego's courage when they could have easily cowered in fear. Instead, they chose to trust, and in return they were granted supernatural courage in the face of the fire.

Since these three men sought God's uncommon peace in the face of pressure, God promoted them. Their courage got upgraded. He'll do the same for us. He will give us the courage to do greater things with our lives than we ever dreamt we could. He promises this in John 14:12 (NIV) when He says, "Whoever believes in me will do the works I have been doing, and they will do even greater things than these." Even greater works than Jesus? That's the kind of life I want.

Let's take a little assessment of how strong *your* courage is. Ask yourself this: Do you worry about what people think about you more than you worry about what God thinks of you? Do you go to bed at night fretting about whether you should've done this or that? Are you afraid to step out and reach out for a promise God has given you because it seems too hard?

How did your courage measure up? Let me say this as clearly as possible: This Kingdom trait is a *must*. You simply *have* to have courage in order to walk into your destiny. If you're struggling with a lack of courage, remember John 16:33 and take heart! You may be in the midst of a battle, but you've already won the war. As long as you stick with Jesus, you'll run off the battlefield victorious. When we choose peace in the midst of chaos, we will find new confidence, clarity, and courage to face any and every situation.

Let's decide today to continue to keep our focus on peace, no matter how many times we have to get our hearts and minds focused on Him again. Remind yourself that God is greater, and fix your focus on His peace. When you do, your life will be upgraded. You'll have the *confidence* to trust Him, the *clarity* to see what He sees, and the *courage* to help you walk boldly in your destiny.

CHAPTER 11

UNCOMMON POWER

According to a 2014 study by the Pew Research Center, 70.6 percent of the American population identified itself as Christian. That's a lot of people. There's no doubt that Christianity is a well-known religion globally, but there's one part of it that—or maybe I should say one person who—is often left out. Some find this too hard to grasp; others find it impractical, and so they discount it. What we are going to talk about is the part that most alters our daily lives. While salvation changes our eternity, discovering the power of the Holy Spirit changes our lives on earth.

Throughout Scripture, we find that God is one being with three aspects—God the Father, God the Son, and God the Holy Spirit. This is known as the Trinity. *Tri-* (meaning three) and *unity* (the idea of being in union). They are three aspects of the same entity but all personalities of the same God. Through the trinity, we see that God's not just into addition; He's into multiplication as well: 1+1+1= 3 but 1x1x1= 1! Just as water can show itself in the form of water, steam and ice—all the same substance, just different aspects—so it is with God. He reveals Himself as the Father, the Son, and the Holy Spirit, three distinct persons in one being.

The Holy Spirit is absolutely essential to fulfilling God's call for us on the earth. *When God fills us with His Spirit, we gain the opportunity to lead supernatural lives.* This is the uncommon power of the Spirit available for every believer. Romans 1:16 (NIV) says, "For I am not ashamed of the gospel, because it is the power of God that brings salvation to everyone who believes: first to the Jew, then to the Gentile." The *power of God* mentioned here is what comes when we *acknowledge* and *understand* the reality of the Holy Spirit. He is the key that unlocks the door to the supernatural in our lives, and God's plan for all of us is to walk in the supernatural daily. I have found that there are three main aspects of the power of the Holy Spirit for everyday living: to *walk* in His will, to *share* Christ with boldness, and to *live* a supernatural life.

Walk: We all want to know why we're here. We want a full explanation from God about our purpose so that we can fulfill it. Who doesn't want to hear those sought-after words, "Well done, my good and faithful servant"?

This is one reason why Rick Warren's *The Purpose-Driven Life* was such a big hit, and why many people scour self-help shelves in bookstores. They're looking for answers about their purpose and destiny. Do you know Who has those answers? Yep! The Holy Spirit does. John 14:26 (ESV) says, "But the helper, the Holy Spirit, whom the father will send in my name, will teach you all things, and bring to your remembrance all things that I said to you."

He will teach and bring to your remembrance what He taught. I love the way 1 Corinthians 2:10-13 describes it in The Message, "The Spirit, not content to flit around on the surface, dives into the depths of God, and brings out what God planned all along. Whoever knows what you're thinking and planning except you yourself? The same with God—except that He not only knows what He's thinking, but He lets us in on it. God offers a full report on the gifts of life and salvation that he is giving us. We don't have to rely on the world's guesses and opinions. We didn't learn this by reading books or going to school; we learned it from God, who taught us person-to-person through Jesus, and we're passing it on to you in the same firsthand, personal way."

Are you struggling to find your purpose? Ask the Holy Spirit. He literally dives into the depths of our Father to reveal His perfect plan for our lives. He will deliver the message to you and empower you to walk it out with confidence.

Share: The second way the Holy Spirit empowers us is by giving us boldness to share our faith with others. In Acts 1:8 (NIV), Jesus told the disciples, "But you will receive power when the Holy Spirit comes on you; and you will be my witnesses in Jerusalem, and in all Judea and Samaria, and to the ends of the earth."

When I was in Bible school, I heard this truth for the first time—that I would receive boldness from the Holy Spirit to share the gospel. One day, I wanted to try it out. I went to a nearby hospital and sat in the waiting room. I silently prayed for God to use me to help someone there whether by prayer or encouragement. As I prayed I felt the Holy Spirit impress on my heart that I should go talk to a certain family.

"I know you don't know me, and I don't know you," I began. "But would you mind if I prayed for you?" The family agreed, so after listening to their needs, I said a prayer over them. When I was done, another lady walked over to me. "My mother is very sick. Would you come to her room with me and pray for her?" I was excited but could feel my nerves. This confidence was not my personality! The Holy Spirit was giving me boldness I couldn't explain. I entered the room and found 13 other people, all gathered around the mother's bed. I felt that we should all get in a circle and pray. After we prayed, the Holy Spirit told me to explain salvation to them and offer to lead them in the prayer.

I was nervous, but with that unexplainable boldness, I did it anyway. The Holy Spirit always knows what needs to be done. ALL 13 people gave their hearts to Christ in that moment! Yes, all of them—I couldn't believe it. It would have been easy to be afraid of what these people might have thought of me, but I relied on the power of the Holy Spirit, and He showed up. He always does. I later found out that that mother was the only Christian in her family. She was always trying to lead her family to Jesus, but they never listened. Still, she kept planting seeds. Those seeds finally sprouted that day, and she entered Heaven peacefully a short time later, knowing that she would see her family again one day! How awesome is our God? Only the power of His Spirit can do things like that.

You might be thinking, "But Caleb, I am not a good communicator. I don't know enough about the Bible. Honestly, I'm not even that good of a Christian!" Paul felt a similar way. In 1 Corinthians 2:4-5 (NIV) he wrote, "My message and my preaching were not with wise and persuasive words, but with a demonstration of the Spirit's power, so that your faith might not rest on human wisdom, but on God's power." He knew that he couldn't convince people of the power of God by His own talents and abilities. He needed the power of God. *He wasn't trying to impress them with what He knew; he was trying to impact them with Whom he had.* When we do the same, there's no doubt in my mind—lives will be changed.

Live: The final way that the Holy Spirit empowers us in our daily lives is by letting us experience the supernatural in our daily circumstances. The reality is that for God, the supernatural is natural, even though that's not the case for us. While He is infinite, we are finite. Sometimes, our minds can't grasp all our spirits know to be true.

In Acts 3, we find an example of the Holy Spirit at work in the life of Peter. One day, he and John were going up to the temple for the regularly scheduled time of prayer. As they started toward the temple, they saw a man who had been lame from birth being carried to the gate. Every day, he would be set there by his friends to beg from those going into the temple. When Peter and John passed him, he asked them for money. Peter's response in verses 5-6 (NIV) is epic, "Look at us!" So, the man turned his body toward them, expecting to receive some money. Peter continued, "Silver or gold I do not have, but what I do have I give you. In the name of Jesus Christ of Nazareth, walk."

Peter then took the beggar by the right hand, helped him up, and instantly his feet and ankles were strengthened. The former beggar jumped up and began to praise God throughout the temple. When people saw the miracle, they started running to Peter and John, as if they were some type of god. Peter responded in verse 12, "Fellow Israelites, why does this surprise you? Why do you stare at us as if by our own power or godliness we had made this man walk?" He then went on to explain that it was through the Spirit's power that the lame man was healed. Friends, that's the type of supernatural life we are all called to lead. One in which we don't shrink back in fear, but we stand up with courage that the Holy Spirit will release supernatural power in our lives. With that power, nothing is impossible. It's not just something from the past; it's for now! It's for today.

As Romans 8:11 says that the same spirit that raised Christ from the dead lives in you. If you're a believer, then you have that Holy Spirit power inside of you already. All you have to do is activate it! John 14:12 (NIV) says, "Very truly I tell you, whoever believes in me will do the works I have been doing, and they will do even greater things than these." How exciting is that? Thanks to the presence and power of the Holy Spirit in our lives, we can see healings, miracles, and prophecies each and every day! We can walk in the same authority that Jesus did and see God's power work in the lives of the people around us.

To do this though we need to quit trying to understand a supernatural God with our natural minds. We never will. It takes faith. In what areas do you need to see the Holy Spirit's power? In finding your purpose? In sharing the gospel with boldness? In your daily circumstances? Today, confess that you have favor with God and man. Confess that He is leading you into a supernatural, power-filled life. Confess that He is revealing His purpose to you, and that you are being empowered to share His love with others.

God made this life to be *supernatural*—and the Holy Spirit is the one that makes this possible. We are called to live uncommon lives. Jesus reminded us in John 16:13 that the Holy Spirit will guide us and show us things to come. So today, trust and rely on the infallible power of the Holy Spirit.

CHAPTER 12

UNCOMMON CHARACTER

Several years ago, Haiti experienced one of the most devastating natural disasters known to man. An earthquake shook the country until almost everything had been destroyed. My wife, her mother, and I visited the country shortly afterward. While there, we visited with our friends who are also founders of Love a Child—an organization with a big heart for orphans. They take care of all the needs of many precious children.

As we sat down to breakfast, our friends told us their account of the earthquake. They had been in their house when it began. It was so intense that they compared it to a rollercoaster. Their home was moving left and right, up and down, throwing them in different directions. Of course, they were terrified. Once the earthquake and all the aftershocks had stopped, they went out to assess the damage to the property. Amazingly, there wasn't a crack in any of their buildings.

"How is that possible? Wasn't everything else in the area destroyed completely?" I asked. "Yes," they replied. "It was because of our foundation." When they were building the structure, they had followed the typical Haitian standard until the Holy Spirit spoke to them to change the plans. "You need to dig a little deeper for the foundation," He whispered to them. So, they went against the industry norm and built their foundation deeper than usual. It cost them almost twice the money, but they moved forward anyway because they knew God had spoken. Sure enough, in the end, it was worth it.

Building a deeper foundation doesn't just build stronger buildings, it builds stronger lives as well. This foundation can be the difference between your success and failure. It can make the difference not just for *you*, but for others who need a strong foundation just as badly. In many years of ministry, I have watched too many lives get destroyed due to a lack of a firm foundation, while other people emerge from the fiercest of storms still standing strong. So, how is your foundation? Is it strong, or has it been built shallow and unstable? Is it made to last, or will it crumble in troubled winds?

If you're unsure, let's use a word that is interchangeable with foundation—character. How's your character? Character is what we build our lives upon. It's character that keeps our lives together when everything around us is falling apart. I've often heard that character is who you are when no one else is looking. I envision character as who I am when I'm going to bed at night, driving in my car by myself, or sitting in my office alone. It's who I am when I have conversations with God or with my wife. It's who I am on stage in front of thousands of people. Character is what's ingrained inside of you—not just what everyone else perceives about you.

There is often confusion between reputation and character. Abraham Lincoln, one of America's greatest presidents, described it best when he said, "Reputation is the shadow, but character is the tree that casts the shadow." Character reveals what's already inside of you. Sure, you probably already have a reputation, but that reputation is based on things that your character has portrayed. If you want to change some aspect of your reputation, you first need to adjust your character. You will need to re-excavate and rebuild on a firmer foundation. So, let me ask you again. How's your foundation? There are times in all of our lives when we need to dig deeper. Like my friends, it may cost us a little more, but it's always worth it.

Character or Compromise

As we begin our digging, I've got some good news, and I've got some bad news. Let's take the good news first. No matter how weak your character is today, it can be strengthened. That's great news, right? You can be a person of uncommon character in our generation! What's the not-so-good news? It always takes time. And time is often the greatest enemy to our success, because we don't have patience. We want to see results, and we want to see them *now*. *It's in the lapse of time between the beginning and the end that the battle for character is waged and won.*

One of the reasons it seems to take so much time is because God always works on the inside first. He won't ask for your hand or your foot before He asks for your heart. Your heart is what decides your character, and your character is what sustains everything else about you. As we focus on what God's doing on the inside, little by little, we'll start to see the fruit on the outside. *Life will give you two roads you can follow—the path to character or the path to compromise. The more often you choose character, the stronger and faster your foundation will be built.*

In Paul's letters to Timothy, he explains this idea. Paul had lived a lot of life by this point, and Timothy was just a young man, full of faith and passion for pursuing God. In 1 Timothy 4:16, he writes, "You influence through your teaching and through your life, so keep a close watch on yourself, and stay true to what is right." Shortly after this, he encourages Timothy again, "Stay true to what's right. Guard your influence, do the things that you've been taught, and follow what the Word says. Then everything will be well." In other words, "Stay true to the things you know, Timothy. Check your foundation on a continual basis. Keep your foundation deep, and you will stand strong."

Friends, I want to encourage you in the same way. Stay true to the things you know to be true about God. Stay true to the promises you find in His Word. As you do, you'll build your foundation stronger. No adversity will be able to undermine your foundation. Your character will be too strong. The truth is that we can't always predict what will happen to us in life, but we can always choose which path we will take. In every situation, we must choose the path of character over the path of compromise. If we do it long enough, it becomes a habit. Pretty soon, our automatic response will be to choose integrity.

Let me say it this way: Adversity will never decide your character; it will reveal it. What you're really made of will come to the forefront. So, strengthen your character in this season, and when the time of testing comes, you'll be prepared. You'll step into your fight confidently. You won't be tossed around with the wind; instead, you'll be able to stand strong and weather the worst of storms.

The Character Challenge

Sometime back I took some teenagers on a mission trip to Italy. We traveled all over the country, from town to town, ministering in churches and youth camps. One afternoon, we had a few hours of free time, so I let the teenagers go shopping and sightseeing before heading to our next ministry site—Greece. I decided to grab some lunch. Pizza, of course.

After scanning the menu, I ordered a full pizza from behind the counter in my name and then sat down to wait for the meal. After several minutes passed I tried to find ways to pass the time so I gathered menus and tourist pamphlets. *Maybe practicing some Italian will help make this time go by,* I thought. 30 minutes later, nothing. *Hmm... maybe they forgot my name? It doesn't exactly sound Italian.* "Do you have anything for Caleb?" I asked politely. I couldn't understand them, but I could tell what they were saying. "Not yet."

So, back I went to my table. I only had a little time left before I needed to meet the rest of the team to catch our boat to Greece. 30 minutes later, I looked down at my watch again. It had been an hour now. Why hadn't the pizza come? I started to become anxious. After another 30 minutes passed, I couldn't sit still any longer. I got up, stood right next to the counter, and every three to four minutes, would ask about my pizza.

"Where's my pizza? I have to go." I sounded like a broken record. I knew I was irritating the people, and I didn't even care. People started staring. Finally, they brought the pizza and put it on the counter. By that point, I was so mad that I let the cashier lady have it. It wasn't her fault, and I knew it, but I let it out anyway.

I know what you're thinking. Aren't you in ministry? Yes, I am. Bear with me. I finally made it to the designated spot, grabbed a slice of pizza and handed the rest to the teenagers. I felt so accomplished—like such a great leader, so well prepared and making it just in time. Another 30 minutes later, the Holy Spirit began to convict me. "What in the world are you doing?" He asked. "Well, I'm heading to Greece...on a mission trip... feeding all these kids...." I shuffled for my answer. "No. What in the world are you doing—acting like that?" He asked more sternly this time.

Then, no joke. He said, "There's something wrong with you." I don't know if you've ever had God tell you there is something wrong with you, but I have had Him tell me that more than once. I guess He knows it gets my attention. At that moment, I realized that there was an aspect of my foundation—my character—that needed fixing. And I needed Him to help me to do this.

It's when we face a problem that our character is revealed. Obviously, I had some patience issues I needed to work on. I had chosen the path of compromise over the path of character more times than I should have throughout my life, and in that moment, it had been revealed, not just to me but also to everyone around me. With character, we'll never be fully where we want to be, but thank God, we don't have to stay where we used to be. He always helps us move forward.

There are things God wants to work out in all of us, and sure, there might be times when you miss it. But when you do and the Holy Spirit speaks to you, be sensitive and allow Him to correct those areas. He's not trying to make your life worse. He's trying to make it better because He knows there will be another pizza lady in your future. There will be another doctor's report. There will be another financial statement or another argument with your spouse. And next time, He wants you to handle it well. Instead of people saying, "What's wrong with him?" He wants people to ask, "What's different about him?"

Evaluate Your Environment

Psalm 1:1-3 (ESV)says, "Blessed is the man who walks not in the counsel of the wicked, nor stands in the way of sinners, nor sits in the seat of scoffers; but his delight is in the law of the LORD, and on his law he meditates day and night. He is like a tree planted by streams of water that yields its fruit in its season, and its leaf does not wither. In all that he does, he prospers. "The tree in this passage is stable because of where it is planted. It sits by a life-giving source, in a life-giving environment. We're healthier and our foundation is stronger when we, too, are planted in a life-giving environment—when we surround ourselves with life-giving people in life-giving places.

What's the environment of your life like? Are you surrounded by negativity, or are you surrounded by people who build you up? We tell our kids that relationship choices matter, but do we tell ourselves this as well? With whom you surround yourself matters at 25, 45, even 75—just as much as it does at 15. *When you plant yourself in life-giving places, you produce fruit in every season and your faith stays strong.*

At this point in history, a lot of people are withering in our world. They're falling to the wayside. Scripture promises that we don't have to. It says that we can prosper in the midst of adversity, but we must evaluate our environment and choose an atmosphere for growth. Let's say that I picked up a beautiful palm tree from Fiji and re-planted it in Denver. It would look pretty for a while, but eventually it would start to wither. The leaves would start to droop. Soon enough, it would die next to all of the evergreen trees.

The difference isn't the tree; it is the place where it was planted. It's the same with our lives. *When we are planted in the right soil, we'll grow. When we are planted in the wrong soil, we'll wither.* As we change our environments, our thoughts will change. As our thoughts change, our habits change. As our habits change, our character changes. And as our character changes, our foundation is strengthened. Of course, the opposite is true as well.

In 2 Chronicles 20, we learn about a godly king named Jehoshaphat. God gave him great victory early in his life because he was planted in the right environment. Toward the end, however, he developed an unhealthy relationship with King Ahaziah. They entered into a covenant for military and business purposes. The Bible describes Ahaziah as a wicked man. Jehoshaphat allied himself with a man of questionable character. This one decision detoured the rest of Jehoshaphat's life away from God's purposes. Sadly, in 2 Chronicles 20:37, Jehoshaphat received a tragic prophetic word, "Because you've allied yourself [because you chose this environment], the Lord is going to destroy your works and all that you've done." As a result, God destroyed everything that he had accomplished up to that point in his life.

This is why Proverbs 12:26 (NIV) says, "The righteous should choose their friends carefully." Choose those who motivate you to obey the Lord. Find people who will unlock your faith and encourage you to honor authority. Spend time with those who will defend you in your absence and inspire you to generosity. *We tend to worry over the future, instead of remembering that the only direct control we have over our future is the seed we sow in the present.* Today, we can work on developing the environment where we are planted by allowing God to build character in us.

Do you need to work on your foundation? Start by putting yourself in faith-filled, positive environments where your life can be enhanced, enriched, and encouraged by excellence in every area. That's the way you're called to live. You're not called to live an average life. You're called to live an uncommon life—built on an uncommon foundation.

CHAPTER 13

UNCOMMON OBEDIENCE

What if I told you that I had the cure to any sickness you could ever contract? What if I said that I held the key to unlock great provision for your life or precise direction for your future? What if I told you that you could take as much as you want of this resource no matter your age or background? And better yet, the doses only increase the positive effects? Sounds too good to be true, doesn't it? I know, but it's not. The best part is that it's completely free! What is this incredible resource? Trust.

I have had to learn and relearn the trust lesson many times in my life. One of the most vivid instances was in 2007. It was right after Sarah and I felt God leading us to move to Asia as missionaries. During my prayer times leading up to our move, I would ask God what He wanted us to do there; however, I never received any solid answer. Then one day, as the time approached, I felt in my spirit that I was to take a preliminary trip to Asia to make arrangements for our upcoming transition. Again, as I prayed, I only received the first step: Book a flight.

In December, I used my airline rewards miles and booked a trip for the following April. Then it was back to waiting. *Anything else, God?* Nope. Silence. Needless to say, I was concerned. I had no meetings planned, no contacts made, no rides from the airport. All I had was a round-trip flight to Asia. I actually started getting a little frustrated with God. "You realize, I am about to move my family around the world for You, and I have nothing set up, right?" I nervously asked.

Then, one day I received the second step: Email the two people He brought to mind that I knew lived in Hong Kong. Initially I was excited until after two weeks, they still hadn't responded. It was now the day before I was set to leave, and I was having some major second thoughts about the trip. I called my dad and asked his advice. He said, "Well, Caleb. If you don't go, you're guaranteed you won't know any more than what you know right now. What is it going to cost you if you go?" My reply of course was time and money. "Well, then. I would be obedient, and trust God to take care of it," he responded.

I knew he was right. The next day, I reluctantly boarded the flight. The entire first flight to Chicago I was worried. When I landed, I rushed to make my connection. Suddenly, I felt my phone vibrate in my pocket. It was an email from one of the individuals I had reached out to. It said, "Caleb, I would love to meet with you the first day you arrive. Let me know when you get here." Do you know what I find interesting? I didn't receive the email when I was praying and crying out to God for direction. I didn't get it in Tulsa, before I boarded my flight. Instead, I received it in the midst of the journey.

Sometimes, I think we are waiting for God to work when He is waiting for us to obey. He's waiting to see if we will trust him to the point where we act first. When I met my contact that first day, he connected me with everyone in Hong Kong that I needed to know within a matter of three hours. *Three hours.* Every door I needed to open was opened for me within that short span of time—through one connection. Still today, I reap the rewards of trusting God on that trip.

What if I hadn't obeyed? What would have happened if I hadn't trusted Him? Isaiah 1:19 says that those who are willing and obedient will eat the best of the land. Obedience is simply having the right attitude paired with the right action. When you do, it allows you to "eat the good of the land," or in other words, to see God's best for your life.

Today you are one step away from everything changing in your life. Take your step of obedience, and watch God unlock the miraculous in your life! In our society, fear and worry run rampant—and for good reason! Everywhere we look, we have a reason to fret for our futures, our finances, our marriages, and our families. As believers, however, we have a guaranteed secret to save us: trust.

Trust is defined as confidence or faith in a person or thing. As believers, we know that our trust is to be in God—our Savior and our Creator. Proverbs 3:5-6 (NIV) is perhaps the best-known verse on the topic. It says, "Trust in the Lord with all your heart, and lean not on your own understanding. In all your ways acknowledge Him, and he shall direct your paths." *Trust in our Father is the only thing that can get us through anything.* The hard part is that trust often makes no sense to us. That's because only God can see the end from the beginning. He can see our lives two months, years and decades from now all in the same moment. To Him there is no difference between the end of our lives and the end of time. He knows what's best for us in every situation. At the moment, it may seem like we know the best option, but we can rest assured that His plan is always better.

A great example of this is found in the story of Abraham in Genesis chapters 12-22. God called him to leave his family in Haran and go to a different place. There was just one little problem:

God didn't give him the name or location of the place. It took full trust in God for Abraham to pack up his things and convince his wife that they were leaving everything behind for an unknown journey for an unknown period of time to reach an unknown destination. Still, he went. And God provided for Abraham in spectacular fashion—even during famine. He gave him a son at a seemingly impossible age. God made the man of faith incredible promises that are still blessing the world today. All because he chose to trust God even when it didn't make sense.

The New Normal

For Abraham, trusting became a new normal. It turned into a lifestyle, not an event. And his life announced the reward of His obedience. God wants to bless us, too. He is looking for people who will trust Him consistently, not just every once in a while.

When I was growing up, my father would often try to sneak little life lessons into everyday activities. Every time I smell paint, I'm reminded of one of those lessons. When he was teaching me to paint, he always said, "Use a dropcloth, so you don't spill on the carpet." I always listened—except for one brief period of time. I was painting at a house, not under the supervision of my dad. I thought about his advice but decided it would be okay not to listen just this "one" time. Sure enough, I did a good job, and nothing spilled on the carpet. I was pretty proud of myself. On the next job, I decided to do the same thing since it had gone so well the first time around. This cycle continued job after job, until one day, my bad habit caught up with me. As I was painting, the entire roller broke and fell onto the carpet. It caused a huge mess—one that I had to pay for! If I would've trusted my dad's advice, making it a lifestyle and not just a one-time event when it was convenient, it would've saved me a lot of explaining (and some money, too)!

Many times, this is what we do with God. We start out trusting Him, but soon enough, we get comfortable with our own abilities and stop seeking His counsel daily. Sadly, like the ruined carpet, it will catch up with us eventually. This lifestyle change comes down to a heart change. One's heart has to say, "I need you, God. I can't do this on my own," and it has to repeat that every day of a person's life. Friends, trusting God works. It's the cure-all for every situation, but it's got to become something we choose daily, not just when it's convenient. If we want uncommon results in our lives, we have to choose uncommon trust—trust that doesn't make sense. Sure, this uncommon trust may require uncommon patience and obedience, but it always produces uncommon joy.

Keep Standing

About 20 years ago, I had a vision that I have never forgotten. I was sitting in Word Explosion, an annual conference at our home church, Victory Christian Center in Tulsa. Suddenly, I saw a picture of myself preaching all over the world. I thought to myself, *How is this going to happen? And when?!* In the natural, it seemed crazy. I was a freshman in college, and at the time, my sermons were only reaching fourth and fifth grade boys in Sunday school. I could not see how I would possibly be preaching to thousands of people overseas.

Still, I knew this was a promise from God, and I have learned that a promise requires a fight before it becomes a reality. You have to hold steady in your faith, no matter what happens as you wait for God to fulfill it. I kept that vision in my heart for years. I genuinely trusted God with it. When my circumstances contradicted it and when doubt tried to fill my mind, I forced myself to remember what I had seen. Somehow, some way I knew He would eventually bring it to pass.

Several years later, I stood in the pulpit during my first evangelistic outreach. As I did, I looked back in my mind's eye to that 19-year-old boy at the altar, choosing to trust God. I could see that young man choosing uncommon patience, placing his hope in the promise that God had given him. Years had passed between that moment and this one. I learned a valuable lesson that day. Our dreams usually don't come to pass overnight, but they will come to pass if we hold tenaciously to God's promises. Hebrews 10:23 (NIV) says, "Let us hold unswervingly to the hope we profess, for He who promised is faithful." No matter what you're going through today, hold onto the vision that God has given you. You may not know when or how it will come to pass; just trust that it will. God always makes a way. His timing is perfect.

Step Out

Sometimes, trust requires you to sit still; sometimes, it requires you to step out. There will be many times you have to wait patiently. In other instances you have to step out obediently. Like Abraham, you may even have to set out for the promise to a destination that isn't exactly clear. *The truth about trust is that it doesn't just prove itself through attitude; it also proves itself through action.*

We see this displayed in Joshua 6. The Israelites were in a battle for Jericho, a city that God had told them was meant to be theirs. Practically speaking though, it seemed there was no way they could conquer Jericho's army. Plus, its city walls were high, and the Israelites were far outnumbered. In verse 2, God gave Joshua a battle plan: Walk around the city one time for six days, and then seven times on the last day. On the final lap, they were to shout and blow their trumpets. The walls would fall, and the city would be theirs. Talk about an uncommon strategy! Joshua operated in uncommon obedience, and sure enough, the walls fell.

When we trust God's plan over our own, even to the point of action, no wall, army, or challenge can keep us from His promise. As we listen to God's words, and then take action with patience, walls fall down, barriers break, and obstacles are removed. Let me remind you that *worry is not a sign of care*. It is a sign of fear. If you keep yourself up at night worrying, take a dose of trust. Trust—demonstrated through attitude as well as action—will cause the walls surrounding your breakthrough to collapse. And like Isaiah 1:19 says, the willing and obedient will always eat the best of the land.

A Gift: Uncommon Joy

When we fully trust Jesus in attitude and action, the result is beautiful: uncommon joy—one that doesn't even make sense naturally speaking. That means people will look at our circumstances and think, *How are they so happy?* In moments like those, the gospel can truly shine. *A believer living with joy in the midst of trials is the greatest witness.*

Take the apostle Paul for example—one of the greatest witnesses of all time. Because he trusted God, both in attitude and action, he experienced uncommon patience and obedience in the midst of shipwreck, persecution, and even unwarranted jail time! During one of his greatest trials, he penned 2 Corinthians 5:6-7 (MSG): "That is why we live with such good cheer. You don't see us drooping our heads or dragging our feet! Cramped conditions down here don't get us down. They only remind us of the spacious living conditions ahead. It is what we trust in but do not yet see that keeps us going."

No matter what you're facing today, God wants to help you in the midst of your situation. As we obey what God has said in the past, we put ourselves in a position to experience God's purpose revealed in the present. Uncommon people don't just believe uncommon things; they also take uncommon actions that produce uncommon results in their lives.

CHAPTER 14

UNCOMMON GRACE

W e were in Tando on the outskirts of Manila in the Philippines focused on reaching some of the most impoverished people in the city. Our team was preaching near one of the city garbage dumps to the poorest of the poor. As I gave the altar call that night, several drug addicts came forward to respond to Christ's message of grace. After we prayed for them, we encouraged them that God had a plan to use their lives to make a big impact for His Kingdom. Several of these young men joined the local church, went through discipleship, enrolled at a local Bible school, and became leaders in the church. Today they lead major ministries in the area. Drugs told them there was no future for their lives; Jesus saw a different outcome—the result of His uncommon grace.

Hopefully, your life has already tasted Christ's grace. Our Heavenly Father gave us the ultimate gift when He, by grace, sent His Son to die for us. Ephesians 2:8 says that it is by grace we have been saved. It's nothing we could manufacture in our own strength. We are incapable of earning it or deserving it. God's grace encountered us in our sin and brokenness and gave us a fresh start to know God and experience His love. It is heaven's free gift to transform our lives. This is the greatest gift we will ever receive, and not just because it changes our lives for eternity—but because it continues to change our lives *today*.

Paid in Full

About a week before our third wedding anniversary, I told Sarah to find a nice dress because I was taking her somewhere special to celebrate. I had been saving some money for a while so that I could take her to a really nice restaurant—one definitely out of our young-couple-with-a-newborn budget.

I remember looking at the menu thinking, *This one meal could buy us a month's worth of diapers. What am I doing?!* Yet, I had it in my heart to show my wife how special she was to me, so I just smiled and acted as carefree as possible. At the end of our meal, the waiter handed us our bill. When I finally worked up the nerve to look at it, there were letters where the numbers should have been. They said, "Paid in Full." I was a bit confused at first because I knew I hadn't given him any money yet.

I looked around. I didn't know anyone else in the restaurant, so surely someone else wouldn't have paid. I motioned for the waiter to come back. "I think maybe there was a mistake." I started to explain. "No, sir," he replied. "Your bill has been paid for. There was a couple here earlier who paid for it. They said they didn't know you; it was just on their hearts to cover your bill tonight." I couldn't believe what I was hearing. My heart soared with gratitude. "Well, let me give you a tip then," I said, fumbling in my pocket for a few bills. "No, sir. They took care of me, too," he replied.

That was the best anniversary dinner ever! I blessed Sarah with an expensive meal, and it didn't cost me anything. I often think of this story when talking about grace, because this is what His grace has done in our lives. It paid the bill of our sin in full.

All of it. Not just some sins or certain generational issues. All of it. Grace is more than just keeping us from getting the punishment that we deserve; it also releases the full measure of God's blessings that we didn't deserve. Jesus demonstrated this uncommon grace for us when He gave His life on the cross for our sins so that we could have a relationship with His Father. That's the grace of salvation, and if you've never received His gift, I would love to lead you in a prayer of salvation. Please turn to the back of the book and read it with me.

Besides the grace He offers us through salvation, He also offers us grace for our daily lives. He gives us the grace to live out His purpose and to love those He has given us. Jesus is the way, the truth, and the life. We no longer have to go through life searching for what we need. He is the solution to every problem and difficulty we may face. We can try other means, but we'll never experience life the way Jesus intended without His uncommon grace.

The Intersection

There's something about driving up to an intersection in unfamiliar territory that makes me a little nervous. I guess maybe it's because I know a decision will have to be made soon. I will either have to turn left, right, or go straight, and often, I don't know which way to go until seconds before I do it. All intersections are crossroads that require a choice. To end up at the destination you're trying to reach, you have to make the *right* choice.

Grace is the intersection of our lives and God's plan. Whether we choose to go God's way or keep driving in our own direction is up to us, but I can tell you that choosing the way of grace usually makes the journey much quicker and more enjoyable. Going our own way brings a lot more missed turns and regrets. When we choose to live every day in God's grace, our lives are changed. They don't magically become perfect, but we are given supernatural strength to face every challenge. Are you on the grace road today? Or have you taken your own path? No matter how fast you're going, it's never too late to turn around.

In Luke 19, we read the story of Zacchaeus. He was a tax collector during Jesus' lifetime, which meant that he was one of the most hated people in all of Israel. And it wasn't just because it was his job to take other people's money. Zacchaeus was dishonest. He was a greedy man, and everyone knew it. One day, Jesus was teaching near his house, and Zacchaeus wanted to see who was talking. Since he was short in stature, he climbed a tree to get a better view. Amazingly, while teaching the people, Jesus pointed to Zacchaeus. "Come down from the tree," he said. "I would like to eat at your house today."

Everyone was shocked. Jesus? Going to the home of one of the worst sinners? People couldn't believe it. Was Jesus aware of what this man had done? No respectable person wanted anything to do with a tax collector, especially not this one. Jesus knew that Zacchaeus was at an intersection moment. He was going to have to decide which way to go. Thankfully, he chose the grace road. That day, he repented of his sins, gave back more than what he had stolen, and received amazing grace. His whole household entered into Christ's uncommon grace as well! From that point forward, Zacchaeus encountered grace, not only for eternal salvation, but also for everyday life.

Praying a prayer of salvation is just the starting point of this journey into grace. We are grateful that Jesus loves us just the way that we are, but He absolutely refuses to leave us that way. How does he move us from "glory to glory" (2 Corinthians 3:18, NASB) and strength to strength (Psalm 84:7, NIV)? By daily giving us the opportunity to experience a fresh inflow of His uncommon grace. So many people view grace as a one-time moment, but that is a faulty understanding of the grace of God. Did you know that Jesus grew in grace? If Jesus, as God's perfect son, experienced greater dimensions of grace in His life, don't you think that you should too?

Hello From the Other Side

Now that we understand grace is more than a one-time transaction, I have a question for you. What are you going to do with what Jesus has done for you? What *does* He want us to do? In short, *freely we've received, so freely we should give.* When we look at people in tough situations, we shouldn't abandon them in their time of need. We should reach out to them in love, with wisdom and practical resources so that they can experience the same grace that we have.

If you listen to music at all, you've probably heard the famous singer Adele's song "Hello." In it she thunders, "Hello from the other side...."When I first heard the song, I liked it. Immediately, though, I tied it to another story I had locked away in my Sunday school memory: the story of the Good Samaritan.

This was a parable Jesus used to emphasize that there will be people in our paths that need us to reach out to them. Just as the Good Samaritan exhibited uncommon grace in this story, so Christ is calling us to go and do the same. Luke 10 tells us that Jesus had just conveyed to an expert of the law the importance of "loving his neighbor." In total shock the man asked, "Who, then, is my neighbor?" Jesus responded with this story.

There was a man going down from Jerusalem to Jericho when robbers attacked him. They stripped him of his clothes, beat him, and left him half-dead on the side of the road. A priest passed him and crossed over to the other side, not wanting to get involved. Then, a Levite, also high in the religious system of the day, crossed over to the opposite side of the road. Finally, a third man came down the road. He was a Samaritan, considered to be a spiritual outcast and social misfit. The Jews hated people from Samaria. The contrast Jesus is setting up in this story can't be overlooked. The people who *should* have helped the man are the priest and Levite—not the Samaritan. Yet, the Bible says that only the Samaritan crossed over to help.

He bandaged his wounds, put the man on his donkey, and took him to an inn so he could recover. He paid the man's wages and instructed the innkeeper, "Look after him, and when I return, I will reimburse you for any extra expense you may have." Jesus then ends the story with a question, "Which of these three do you think was a neighbor to the man who fell into the hands of the robbers?" The expert replied, "The one who had mercy on him." The chapter ends with a simple admonition from Jesus, "Go and do likewise."

Let me ask you this: Have you ever felt you were in a season where you were on the other side? Like no one understood or cared about you? Usually this is more of an internal loneliness than an external one, but it can happen either way. We all go through hard times, often feeling marginalized and forgotten. That's a strategy of the enemy. He uses isolation to make us think we're alone. I'm so glad that God remains faithful during these times; He will send people like the Good Samaritan down our path to help us through tough times. In so doing, these people become channels of Christ's grace toward us. Yet we must make sure that we aren't just grace consumers. We are called to be grace contributors as well. It's up to us to reciprocate what has been poured into our lives. *The beautiful thing about pain is that it always has a purpose.* After you have been on one side, you can better help someone else who is experiencing the same thing. *Once you've received grace, it's much easier to give it.*

There are three main takeaways I want us to identify from this story—three ways we are to extend grace, just as the Good Samaritan did.

The first is that the Samaritan maintained his *focus.* He saw the man for who he was, not for what he had been through. He didn't pull out a questionnaire or ask him where he was from to decide if he had deserved the beating. That didn't matter to him. He knew that no matter what had happened in the past, God still loved the beaten man and had a plan for him.

The second is that the Samaritan extended *compassion* to the man. *Compassion is not pity that looks down on someone; it's a change of heart that allows you to see a person as God does.* I'm sure part of the Samaritan's compassion came from the fact that he could identify with what this man was going through. He had been rejected and marginalized his whole life, but I believe that at some point, he had been shown grace. And, he knew what a difference it could make.

The third is that the Samaritan *took action.* He let his compassion move him to do something. This final part is what makes grace so uncommon. Jesus didn't just look down from heaven and see our wickedness and pity us. No! He entered the story and took action because of the great compassion He had towards humanity. This is what makes the lasting impact.

Friends, God wants us to live with this kind of grace. This is our moment to call out from the other side and be a helping hand, regardless of past, present, or future. This uncommon grace is what life is all about. It *is* the gospel. We must not allow our faith to simply be a fictional story from the past or history recorded in a book. Let's make it a way of life. Today, decide what you will do with the sacrifice Jesus paid. Ask yourself, "What will *I* do with the gospel?" And from now on, in each and every moment, choose uncommon grace.

CHAPTER 15

CHOOSING THE UNCOMMON
LIFE DAILY

Any great warrior will tell you that *you don't build your stamina during the battle; you build it before.* Before the battle is training time. During training, you become who you are through your daily routine. When you're consistent in your daily life, you'll be able to face each battle with confidence. And when you know you've trained properly, the battle will no longer intimidate you. So, let's take a minute to recap what we have examined in this book. Let's talk about how we can live an uncommon life, as Jesus did, today.

Uncommon Availability // Being *around* is never enough; we must live each day *available*, allowing God to interrupt our plans. When we choose this trait, we no longer live under the daily pressure of striving to conform to society's expectations, but instead we live by God's standards. As we follow Christ's example we realize that when we make ourselves available, He will make us capable to face anything that comes in life.

Today, make a decision to clear your schedule, surrender your desires, and exchange your plans for God's. When you're consistently available to what God wants to do, He can form you into the person He created you to be. Every day is an opportunity to surrender your time, talent, and treasure to God and watch what He will do through you.

Uncommon Attitude // When we raise our attitude under pressure, our result will rise as well. So, it's attitude—not circumstance—that decides our outcome. Remember Paul? His attitude during trials was one we all need. He was in chains for preaching the gospel, yet he continued to preach it! He chose to see God's promise over his current problem, and this perspective is one God blesses. When things get hard in our daily lives, we should follow the example that we see in God's Word. If we'll remain persistent in seeking God, be Spirit-led in making our decisions, and praise God at all times, we can live with an uncommon attitude.

Uncommon Language // This is the understanding that one's words direct the course of one's life. The longer you live, the more you'll find that it's hard to live in victory when you're talking defeat. Choose words that lead you toward your destiny, not your demise. You can never go wrong by speaking God's Word!

When we choose common words—words that simply describe our situation—we find ourselves living lives that are less than God's best. But when we choose words that are uncommon—words of faith, words of hope, words that describe what God sees about our lives—we create a faith-filled, positive environment. So, today speak faith over fear. Speak God's promises over your problems.

Uncommon Generosity // God is a generous God, and He calls His people to live with uncommon generosity. Generosity connects people in a unique way. When you give, your gift often outlives you. It reaches many more people than you could've ever reached on your own. Uncommon generosity is living life with open hands, open to what God has entrusted to you, open to the opportunities that God has placed before you, and open to the needs that God has placed around you. We are responsible for the things God has entrusted us with. As we live with uncommon generosity we are able to help the hurting, reach the lost, and lift the broken.

When you live with uncommon generosity, God will unlock an uncommon supply over your life. He says in Genesis 8:22 that as long as the earth remains, there will be seedtime and harvest. It doesn't matter how much you have, God can multiply what you give.

Uncommon vision // Proverbs 29:18 (KJV) says, "Where there is no vision the people perish." When there's no dream, hope, or revelation for our lives, we go nowhere. Once we get a clear vision, though, we are inspired with life-changing passion, which produces inspired action. This has little to do with what we see in the natural. It has everything to do with what we see by faith when our eyes are closed.

People with uncommon vision see *promises* instead of *problems*. They see *opportunities* in what everyone else deems *obstacles*. They see supernatural *intervention* in the middle of natural *issues*. When we choose to see what God sees, the direct result will be a greater passion for His purposes. Even in the midst of our darkest hour, He can work. Even in the mundane, He can perform miracles. Make a decision today that you're going to see with eyes of faith. Ask the Holy Spirit to show you what He sees and ask Him to help you live with uncommon vision.

Uncommon pursuit // We possess the things that we consistently pursue. So, every day, we must strive to know God, and then make Him known. Knowing God is not about reading your Bible a few days out of the week and attending church every Sunday. It's about pursuing a relationship with our Father—daily, no matter the cost. Uncommon pursuit is a desire on the inside that is revealed through our choices on the outside. In life, we can pursue many things but often those pursuits lead us to the wrong place. When we pursue a real and personal relationship with God, through the person of Jesus in the power of the Holy Spirit, we will experience supernatural life. Regardless of what you've pursued in the past, make a decision to pursue God and His will over everything else.

Uncommon Faith // Following God is a life of adventure, of joy, and of purpose when we choose faith. Just because God's plans are promised doesn't mean they are automatic. This is the importance of faith. It takes what God has said and applies it to our lives. Faith believes even when we don't see. Faith acts even when we don't know what is on the other side. Throughout the Bible, we read stories of men and women who lived and walked in faith. From Joshua to Gideon to Esther and to David, each helps us to understand that as we follow God, we are called to a journey of faith.

You can be encouraged today regardless of your circumstance. Faith can change any situation. When you walk in faith remembering who is on your side, the Bible promises that anything is possible. Each day, take a step forward: a step of faith, a step toward the purpose and the plan that God has for your life. The Bible reminds us that "the just shall live by faith" (Hebrews 10:38, NKJV). Faith is the currency of the Kingdom of God.

Uncommon Love // The Bible tells us that God is love. Jesus demonstrated this love to us when He came to the earth. He loved everyone. His love wasn't conditional, limited, or emotional. Love is who He was. Jesus showed us the love of God as He chose compassion everywhere that He went. His compassion led Him to action. Ephesians tells us to love as Jesus did, every day.

We're to love wide, reaching out to anyone, no matter how lost, labeled, sick, or sinful. Then we're to love long, walking with them along the road of salvation, healing and helping them to develop their full potential. We're also to love high, teaching others about God's promises and helping them to go after them. Finally, we're to love deep by reaching into the depths of people's hearts, and pulling them out of the pit. Heaven can invade earth through *you* daily, as you seek to love as Jesus did, with an uncommon love.

Uncommon Peace // In life, we all experience seasons that are challenging or difficult. God gives us His promise of peace in everything we experience. Jesus illustrated this throughout His life. In difficult situations, in storms and in tragedy, He showed us that God always brings peace to His people. Today, you can rest in the peace of God. You may be in the middle of a storm or in the middle of a chaotic situation, but when you're rooted in the peace of God, you can have confidence in the midst of the problem.

Take heart because our victory has already been won. When we live in peace, we can face pressure confidently and see God's power push us to promotion. Our confidence, clarity and courage get upgraded, as we daily choose peace, seeing possibilities over problems.

Uncommon Power // While salvation changes our eternity, discovering the power of the Holy Spirit changes our lives on earth. Jesus promised Him to us in John 16:13 (NIV). He said, "When the Spirit of truth comes, he will guide you into all truth. He will not speak on his own but will tell you what he has heard. He will tell you about the future." Today, start developing your relationship with the Holy Spirit. Confess that He is leading you into a supernatural, power-filled life. Confess that He is revealing God's purpose to you, and that you are being empowered to share His love with others. Allow Him to guide you and show you things to come. And in every situation, choose to rely on the power of the Holy Spirit.

Uncommon Character // A person's character is the foundation of his or her life. There are times we all need to dig deeper to ensure that our foundation is stable. In life, it may cost more, but the end result will be well worth it. In our daily routine, we can't get discouraged by the time a foundation requires. As we focus on the unseen, little by little, we will start to see the fruit that God is releasing on the outside.

If you make a decision to strengthen your character today, you'll be ready when the storms of life come. Remember that your environment affects your character, and every day, we have the ability to choose the environment that we place ourselves in. Your environment affects your thinking, your thinking affects your behavior, your behavior forms your habits, and your habits produce results in your life.

Uncommon obedience // Obedience to God is one of the keys to unlocking the miraculous in our lives. Throughout scripture we see examples of men and women who obeyed God no matter the cost. In life it's easy to get caught up with what is easy, but our focus should be on Christ. We need to ask the question, "God, what do you want me to do?" and then obey the answer He gives us. The Bible reminds us that if we are willing and obedient, we will walk into the best that God has for us. Uncommon obedience isn't just a one-time decision; it's a way of life that enables us to walk into uncommon blessing.

Uncommon Grace // Grace is one of the greatest gifts that we will ever receive from God. We can't earn it, and we don't deserve it, but He gives it to us anyway. God's grace enables us to walk in the freedom that He has given us, and it empowers us to live the life that He created for us. God doesn't care how broken you are or how bad your past is. He goes out of His way to bring the worst outcast into His Kingdom. After we have received grace, we have to answer the question: Now what? What are we going to do with what Jesus has done for us? In short, freely we've received, so freely we should give. Like the Good Samaritan, we must keep our focus right, embrace compassion, and let that compassion lead us to action.

I encourage you to regularly take each one of these topics and ask yourself, "How well did I live with uncommon faith today? Did I choose uncommon peace? What about uncommon love?" If you will ask the Holy Spirit to help you live an uncommon life daily, it won't be long before you'll see abundant fruit.

What do you say? Will you join me in the pursuit of uncommon living? Let's choose to seek first the Kingdom of God. Let's be willing to sacrifice. Let's sow seeds for the future. Let's do everything with an excellent spirit. Even in uncommon trials, let's remain confident that on the other side of our deepest pain can come our greatest purpose. Don't be too hard on yourself. You may have to start slow, but just keep going, asking Jesus to keep releasing His uncommon life through you. As long as we're choosing the uncommon, so will He.

DAILY UNCOMMON DECLARATIONS

1. Today, I will keep an uncommon attitude in the midst of every situation because I know that God is for me and is working on my behalf.

"...Being confident of this, that he who began a good work in you will carry it on to completion until the day of Christ Jesus." —Philippians 1:6 (BSB)

2. Today, I choose to live uncommonly available to my Father as He makes me capable to live the life He has called me to.

"And so, dear brothers and sisters, I plead with you to give your bodies to God because of all he has done for you. Let them be a living and holy sacrifice—the kind he will find acceptable. This is truly the way to worship him."—Romans 12:1-2 (NLT)

3. Today, I choose to speak only words of victory that will lead me toward my destiny. I will send my uncommon language ahead of me to create what God has in store for me.

"The tongue has the power of life and death, and those who love it will eat its fruit."—Proverbs 18:21 (NIV)

4. Today, I will live with uncommon generosity, viewing each opportunity to help someone in need through the lens of God's unconditional love towards me.

"One person gives freely, yet gains even more; another withholds unduly, but comes to poverty. A generous person will prosper; whoever refreshes others will be refreshed." —Proverbs 11:24-25 (NIV)

5. Today, I choose to see God's promises over my problems as well as opportunities in what others would call obstacles. I will choose to see life with uncommon vision, trusting that God is working everything together for my good.

"Therefore, since we have so great a cloud of witnesses surrounding us, let us also lay aside every encumbrance and the sin which so easily entangles us, and let us run with endurance the race that is set before us, fixing our eyes on Jesus, the author and perfecter of faith." —Hebrews 12:1-2 (NASB)

6. Today, I will pursue God and His peace above all else. I will spend my days learning to know Him and make Him known, fully trusting that He is working on my behalf.

"But seek first his kingdom and his righteousness, and all these things will be given to you as well." —Matthew 6:33 (NIV)

7. Today, I accept the fact that I will never be "good enough," and that God always will be. So, I put my faith in Him, keeping my confidence that He is always faithful.

"So, do not throw away your confidence; it will be richly rewarded. You need to persevere so that when you have done the will of God, you will receive what he has promised." —Hebrews 10:35-36 (NIV)

8. Today, I choose to love everyone as Jesus does without condition. I will allow Heaven to invade earth through me, as I put compassion into action and love the one in front of me.

"A new command I give you: Love one another. As I have loved you, so you must love one another. By this everyone will know that you are my disciples." —John 13:34-35 (NIV)

9. Today, I will live with a peace that passes all understanding, because I am confident in this: He is bigger than anything I could ever face. When the battle feels too hard, I will take heart, because He has already won the war.

"Then you will experience God's peace, which exceeds anything we can understand. His peace will guard your hearts and minds as you live in Christ Jesus." —Philippians 4:7 (NLT)

10. Today, I claim that I will live in the power of the Holy Spirit. I trust Him to guide me throughout my day and show me things to come.

"But the helper, the Holy Spirit, whom the father will send in my name, will teach you all things, and bring to your remembrance all things that I said to you." —John 14:26 (ESV)

11. Today, I choose to walk down the road to character, building a strong foundation. I will place myself only in life-giving environments, so that I can produce good fruit and keep my faith strong.

"Pay close attention to yourself and to your teaching; persevere in these things, for as you do this you will ensure salvation both for yourself and for those who hear you." —1 Timothy 4:16 (NASB)

12. Today, I acknowledge that trust in my Father is the only thing that can get me through absolutely anything. I will be obedient to anything He asks of me.

"If you are willing and obedient, you will eat the good things of the land." —Isaiah 1:19 (NIV)

13. Today, I declare that I will be a conduit of uncommon grace, freely extending it to others, just as I have freely received it.

"Be merciful, just as your Father is merciful." —Luke 6:36 (NIV)

PRAYER FOR SALVATION

Dear Heavenly Father,

Thank you for your uncommon love that sent Jesus to die for my sins. I believe that He is the only way, the truth, and the life. I ask you to forgive me of my sins, and give me a fresh start in life. I make a decision to live for and honor you with my life. Holy Spirit, I invite you into my life, and I ask you to lead me in every decision that I make. In Jesus' name, Amen.

If this is your first time praying the salvation prayer, congratulations! You have made the best decision anyone can make. And if you rededicated your life to Christ today, I am proud of you, too. I would love to hear your story, as well as the stories of God's continued faithfulness in your life. If you prayed this prayer, or if you have a story of how the truths in this book have impacted you, please reach out on Instagram via @calebwehrli or @_inspireintl. I am praying and believing God's very best for you!